# ULSTER STOCK

# Michael Sheane

ARTHUR H. STOCKWELL LTD.
Torrs Park   Ilfracombe   Devon
*Established 1898*
*www.ahstockwell.co.uk*

British Library Cataloguing-in-Publication Data.
A catalogue record for this book is available
from the British Library.

Arthur H. Stockwell Ltd. bears no responsibility
for the accuracy of events recorded in this book.

By the same author:
*Ulster & Its Future After the Troubles (1977)*
*Ulster & The German Solution (1978)*
*Ulster & The British Connection (1979)*
*Ulster & The Lords of the North (1980)*
*Ulster & The Middle Ages (1982)*
*Ulster & Saint Patrick (1984)*
*The Twilight Pagans (1990)*
*Enemy of England (1991)*
*The Great Siege (2002)*
*Ulster in the Age of Saint Comgall of Bangor (2004)*
*Ulster Blood (2005)*
*King William's Victory (2006)*

ISBN 978-07223-3844-5
Printed in Great Britain by
Arthur H. Stockwell Ltd.
Torrs Park    Ilfracombe
Devon

# Contents

# Chapter 1

## *A Well-Known Name*

The origin of a lot of the Ulster clans has been lost to history, but one name stands out amongst them all – O'Mullan, the name of a tribe common in Ireland. Many people have claimed Irish and Scots-Irish roots, especially the Americans, both Catholic and Protestant. A glance at the map of the northern clans gives us an idea of the geographical location of these little kingdoms. As a County Antrim man I must look at the clans that existed (and still exist) in this part of Ulster. Names like Carrickfergus, Larne, Ballycastle, Rathlin Island, Dunseverick and Dunluce still stand out. Dominating these locations were the Clan MacDonnell of Antrim, who had their headquarters at Dunluce Castle on the north coast of Ulster. Their influence spread inland, and the ancient kingdom of Dalriada fell under their jurisdiction. The MacDonnells eventually built Glenarm Castle, about fifteen miles from the port of Larne in South Antrim. The MacDonnells are still resident at Glenarm, living in a mansion often named Glenarm Castle.

It is difficult to say where one should start writing about not only the Antrim tribes but also those of the entire northern region. It is purposeless to wait until all the information is perfect before publishing, for it would not be worth publishing at all. The professional historian tends to the perfect, whereas the amateur is content with his own collection of data and facts. The O'Mullan name is central in this work and it is my intention to examine all the facts and stories about this Gaelic name, also with the O'Cahan (O'Kane) and O'Mellan. One inevitably falls back and examines the pre-plantation stock in Ulster and their position vis-à-vis the English Crown, with its many attempts to dominate the natives. County Antrim is special, for here there is a close connection with the Scots: MacDonnell at one time dominated the Mull of Kintyre peninsula. These clans bridge religious opinions and beliefs, and they are close to the legends surrounding the clans of the Highlands of Scotland. The home of colonization in Ireland was Ulster: the planters, like the Gaels, liked the green fields and sang their praises.

In County Antrim, as elsewhere in the north, the remains of plantation forts can be seen; for example, Dunseverick on the north coast, whose praises I have already sung. Both Protestants and Catholics in Ulster can unite in their quest for their origins, for the northern Unionist knows that his ancestors were the Scots-Irish of the province and the ancestors of the Catholics were the Gaels. No clan in Ulster shows the internal effects of political and religious divisions more closely than the clans O'Mullan, O'Cahan and O'Mellan.

The Ulster clans were always feuding, carrying off one another's cattle and settling upon the land. The Scots of the Glens of Antrim had their roots in the feuds surrounding the north coast and their castle at Dunluce. Division meant that the English could settle upon the land as well as the MacDonnells from Scotland. However, the English fell to the level of the Gaels and successive laws were passed to stop this process. The Gaels of the Antrim Glens were regarded as barbaric Irishmen, and the MacDonnells were regarded in the same light in English eyes. The river Bann divided the MacDonnell lands from those of central Ulster – the O'Mullans and O'Cahans and the tribes of the Sperrin Mountains. None of these clans had lands as extensive as the MacDonnells of Antrim. The largest kingdom was Tir-Owen, and it is not certain which sept led the way – possibly the Ui Neill. Lough Neagh, also divided County Antrim from Tir-Owen (County Tyrone). West of the Bann flows the river Foyle, flowing into Lough Foyle. Further west is Donegal or Tir-Conail, dominated by the O'Donnells of the Glens.

The Romans had mapped the northern clans, especially those of the east coast of Eirinn (Ireland). They did not attempt to make the short journey between Portpatrick (Scotland) and Donaghadee in eastern North Down. However, it is very likely that the Romans traded with the Gaels from their base in north-east England at Chester on the river Dee. To the Romans the tribes of the Antrim Glens were sunk in barbarism and with the rise of the Catholic Church in the fifth century, there may have been efforts to Christianize Ireland before the arrival of Saint Patrick in 432. The rise of the Gaelic clans in the North is a phenomenon of the growth of the Church in Ireland. The Christianity that the O'Mullan tribe received was that based at Rome, whose head was the Pope. The O'Mullans dwelt between the river Bann and the river Roe, and above them were the scenic Sperrin Mountains. In County Antrim the Antrim Hills rise above the Glens and are the same now as at the time of the MacDonnell clan.

These tribes carried on diplomatic relations with one another – they were not all warlike. The bards or poets of the Glens and Donegal sang the praises of mythical Ireland, where the Milesians or Gaels had settled and where the gods reigned over. The origin of the tribes in the North is entirely Gaelic and the Romans would have regarded the Gaels of Ireland in the same light as the barbaric septs in Europe, for example the Gauls who inhabited what is now present-day France. The clans had no money and trade was carried on by barter. This divided the Roman economy from that of the MacDonnells and the O'Mullans.

It has been noted that the name O'Mullan (with its many varieties, including Mullane) is one of the most common names in Ireland, and is found in nearly every part of Ireland. The Irish O'Maolain is the chief tribe, probably derived from the Gaelic word 'maol', meaning bald or tonsured. There are different districts from which the name is derived. Immigration has complicated the position, for the Gaels had tried to ape the civilization of the invading English. McMullans who had immigrated from Scotland often changed their name to MacMullan, and Mullins from England originate from other roots. There were also deliberate changes of the name – it can be derived from 'mill', for which the Middle English is 'miln' or 'mulne'. We come across Lawrence Mulene (Lawrence of the Mill) in 1278 in Bardsley. It can also come from the French 'de Molines', and this goes back almost certainly to the Norman invasion of England in 1066. In 1841 Lord Ventry's family assumed the name 'de Moleynes' in place of 'Mullins'. This was probably due to political reasons, reversing the change from 'de Moleyns' to 'Mullins'.

There were the Scottish Macmillans, and they present a complicated case. It is almost certain that there were Macmillans in Ulster in the seventeenth century, and had altered the name to Macmillan. There were of course the MacDonnell settlements on the Antrim coast, particularly in the Glens, and this started the colonization process. There came about in Ulster the phenomenon of the Reformation. In the fifth century the inhabitants of Ireland were called Scots. There was also the Dalriada tribe of North Antrim. The Gaelic form of MacMillin and the origins of the name derive from the Gaelic word for tonsure or bald. This points to an original connection between the Irish O'Mullan and the Scots Macmillan. There were numerous settlements of O'Cahans and O'Mullans in Scotland at a much later date. The two-way traffic between Scotland and Ulster made ready the ingredients for an important kingship.

An important sept of the O'Mullan tribe has its origins in County Galway, and the ancestors of the sept are said to have descended from a king of Connaught. O'Mullan of Connaught has a crest of arms. The main feature of the shield is a red hand holding a dagger between three crescents. The Connaught O'Mullans have different origins. Mullans are still rife on the western seaboard, and the best-known family came from

Aran. Pat Mullan was one of a family of Mullans; his father was a fisherman and also worked several acres of land. He made kelp from seaweed and traded in stock. At nineteen years of age, Pat headed for America, but later returned to Aran. Upon this island the 'Man of Aran' was made. He had a daughter, Barbara, who spent her early days in the United States, becoming a famous star on stage, film and television.

In south-west Ireland the name O'Mullan is Mullane. The greatest documentors of the name are the O'Mullan family of Britas, and the land here was loaned out to it at an early date to a John O'Mullane. Dermot O'Mullane of Britas was the grandfather of John O'Mullane who died in 1766. John's daughter Catherine married Morgan O'Connell, and the famous Irish nationalist Daniel O'Connell is said to have been their child. Daniel O'Connell is said to have taken his facial expression from his father's people, the O'Connells. The septs that are mentioned in the study are chiefly the O'Mullan and O'Mellan septs. The O'Mellans were centred around South Derry and North Tyrone, in a territory known as the Meallanact, which included present-day Cookstown. They were to play an important role in the history of Ulster, and they were the hereditary keepers of the Bell of Saint Patrick. In Ulster they have become as important as the O'Mullans. Many of them had their names changed to the more familiar O'Mullan. The name Mallon was also well known. He was the chief of staff of the Irish Citizens Army, and took part in the Easter Rising of 1916.

The Ulster sept of the O'Mullans belongs to County Londonderry, and was a leading sept under the O'Cahans. It was already declining before the plantation/colonization of the province. The troubles of the seventeenth century had a profound effect upon them, and they further declined in influence and importance. The leading light in the Londonderry area (Derry) was the rapparee Shane Crossagh O'Mullan. He had been evicted from his property and had led the life of a highwayman. He was eventually hanged in Derry Jail. Well-known authors have also been descended from the O'Mullans of Tyrone. There is a connection between the two septs, and this goes back to the very early times of Owen, son of the great warrior Niall of the Nine Hostages, who climbed to power in the fourth century AD. Owen had a number of sons, and had obtained Saint Patrick's blessing.

There are two remarkable men of the O'Mullan name that must be mentioned. The first is James Mullin, born at Cookstown, County Tyrone in 1846. He left school when he was eleven and did farm work for sixpence a day, and was a carpenter for nine years. He was one of the first recruits for the Fenian movement, which he joined in 1865. He and his friends were denounced by the Church. At twenty-two years of age, he attended Cookstown Academy, paying his way by part-time work. He graduated in arts at Galway, and he hired himself out to students until he had sufficient funds to start a medical course, which he eventually completed. He was able to practise medicine in London and Cardiff; and at Cardiff Parnell, the great Irish nationalist, stayed with him. He wrote his autobiography. He had become a ship's surgeon and a journalist, writing a great deal.

O'Mullan was therefore a self-made and self-educated man. He was alert to the many renderings of his surname. He mentions that he went to Galway; here the registrar put his name down with an 'i' instead of an 'a'. He spelled his name this way from then on. O'Mullan was a Roman Catholic, but he went to a Protestant school and he remarked that participation in religion was a good idea, enabling young people to understand one another and make friendships. It transcended the religious gulf in Ulster, and bigotry was not tolerated in the school.

The headmaster was the Reverend David Mullan, who had written a number of books, which are in the National Library in Dublin. His works are original, even though you may not agree with his conclusions. His chief work was *The Nature of the Pentecostal Baptism*. In this work, dedicated to the National Library in 1904, is an attempt to draw a parallel between the testing of Israel in history and the testing of the Church, presumably Roman Catholic. The present situation of the Church is likened to the return from Babylon by Israel. The coming of the Messiah is mentioned. He mentions the ideal state of the Church, the Kingdom of God. David Mullan proposed the unity ideal before the Edinburgh World Missionary Conference in 1910, which gave it much publicity. He pointed to the Bible references for unity amongst the churches, namely the seventeenth chapter of John – a goal which ordinary Ulstermen could attain. This goal was only obtainable by a Pentecostal baptism of the Holy Ghost. The O'Mullans of Derry and the O'Mullans of Tyrone are supposed to trace back their origins to the dim past of Irish history, to which the author now turns.

# Chapter 2

## *Movements of the Clans*

It is said that the history of Ireland starts with the High-King Niall of the Nine Hostages, so called because he obtained the pledges from nine nations. He became High-King of Ireland in AD 379, and was tall and fair-haired with blue eyes of Gaelic blood. He was a great warrior, and most of his time was spent in attacking the west coast of Britain, as well as plundering France. It is possible that he had captured Saint Patrick in one of his many raiding expeditions. The slave Patrick herded sheep around Slemish Mountain, near present-day Ballymena, in County Antrim. Niall died in a military fray into France in AD 405.

Niall had eight sons, and one of these, Laeghaire, succeeded his father as High-King of Ireland. He held the high-kingship during Patrick's missionary journey, and tolerated Christianity, although it is not sure whether he received the Catholic Church itself. He presided in battles, and by his own request was buried upright with his face towards his hereditary foes. Two of the other sons of Niall, Eoghan (Owen) and Conall, marched north and conquered north-west Ulster and founded a new state whose capital was Ailech, a fort near present-day Londonderry, and at the southeast of the Inishowen Peninsula. The territory of Conall (now Donegal) used to be known as Tir-Conall (the Land of Conall). The O'Donnells of Donegal were descended from him. The territory of Owen was Inishowen (the Island of Owen), still known by that name. The Clan Owen later expanded into Tyrone (Tir-Owen), the Land of Owen.

From Owen have descended many tribes, clans and names that have figured largely in the history of Ulster – O'Neill, MacLoughlin, O'Cahan, O'Hagan, O'Mullan, O'Mullin and many others.

Information about the dividing of Inish-Owen amongst the tribesmen is derived from *The Tripartite Life of Saint Patrick*. This seems to have been written partly in the ninth century. It has to be used with great caution as a life of Saint Patrick. It described a journey to Inish-Owen, which does not seem impossible, for the apostle was a great traveller. Eugene Mullen's poem says of Patrick 'To all the seven kingdoms thou didst go'. It mentions the primatial see at Armagh, and that God's angel was guiding him. The account describes how Inish-Owen was divided amongst the sons of Owen at a very early date after the death of the King. One may be sceptical about Patrick's activities, but it is likely that the account carries a good deal of truth.

*The Tripartite Life* describes how Patrick blessed the children of Conall. He then went over to Bernes Mor into the country of Owen to Maga Ithc, where he baptized Owen. Patrick blessed Eogan (Owen) with his sons. Murdach was Owen's favourite son, and Patrick said that the kingship would descend from him for ever. Fergus was the next favourite son of Owen and Patrick acknowledges him as a great warrior. One of the sons of Fergus, Coelbad, made a bad beginning, for he expelled Saint Patrick from his territory. The other son, Aedh (Hugh) gave Patrick a great welcome. Patrick then proceeded into the territory of the Bretagh, the district of Owen's son Ailill and ordained Aengus, son of Ailill in that place, Domriach Bili by name.

The hand of Saint Patrick can be traced, for the word Domnach (The Lord's Day or church) is found in place names. There is Domnach Mor Tochair near Carndonagh where the adjacent Glen Tocher preserves part of the name. A look at the map shows Inish-Owen in the north-west while Domnach Bali is now Movelle. The territory of the sons of Fergus embraced Carnhonagh to Doagh and Lough Swilly. These were the lands of the Mulfoyle sept of Clan Fergus. To the south of the lands of Fergus lay the tribal land of Murdach and Ochy Binny, whom Saint Patrick had blessed.

In the century after the death of Saint Patrick, there was a great deal of tribal movement in Ulster. North Antrim stands out, the territory of the Dalriada tribe. The name 'Dal' derives its name from 'descendants of', and Riada was the nickname of a chieftain called Cairbre Righfada (Riada) of the Long Armed. The title 'Dalriada' is still used, but it is more often known as 'The Route'. A descendant of Cairbre Righfada named Fergus travelled over to Scotland in the fifth century and founded the Kingdom of Argyll or Scottish Dalriada. The invading Gaels brought with them their language, and gave their name to the area, for they were Scots or Scoti. The descendants of Fergus became kings of Scottish Dalriada and at length kings of the united kingdom of the Picts of northern Scotland in the reign of the Scottish king, Kenneth MacAlpin. Later in the sixth century, Columba set sail for Iona; he returned to Ulster on several occasions as the arbiter of disputes in the northern region of the province. This was the famous Convention of Drumceat which gathered near Limavady. Later, too, the Scots MacDonnells returned to the Antrim coast and settled in the Glens.

The growth of the Clan Owen is the subject we are concerned with here. From a cradle at the bottom of Inish-Owen the descendants of Owen fanned out in forays to the east and south, a movement that was not swift or overwhelming. These movements can be likened to that of a great glacier that moved forward from the centre in Derryveagh Mountains and the Barnesmore Hills of Donegal. The glacier at length covered the countryside. The first thrust of the Clan Owen was that of the Clan Binny, which has been placed at AD 563. The movement bypassed the land of the Cianachta or Children of Cian, whose name is preserved in the present barony of Keenaught. They swung south-east into County Tyrone, perhaps attacking Clan Binny or making a frontal advance against the Owen clans right to the river Blackwater (or Davel). There were pockets of O'Hamills at Clonteacle on the Blackwater and this may mark the limit of their advance. Clan Binny drove out the Oriella clan from the area west of the river Binny, embracing Coleraine to Lough Neagh, and drove them across the river. The prophecy was that the descendants of Ochy Binny would be warriors. Much information about the Clan Binny is contained in Dr James O'Kelly's *Gleanings from Ulster History*.

The Clan Fergus now came into view, following the advance of Clan Binny. The O'Clery geneaologies point out the descendants of Coelbad son of Fergus, from which many well-known Gaelic names emerge. One sept was Ogain, from which springs the O'Hagans. Another was the Coinne, from which came the O'Quins. Another was the Mael Fobaill, from which are descended a long line of Mulfoyle chieftains. The Mulfoyles were centred around Lough Swilly, and others probed south-east into Tir-Owen (Tyrone) in the wake of the Clan Binny. There were many clerics in the Clan Fergus, but the clan was not wanting in martial arts. Clan Fergus is portrayed as the fighting vanguard of McLoughlin and O'Neill, and they fought their way into Tullyhog and Armagh, to become masters of Tir-Owen.

The royal clans of the province, the O'Neills and McLoughlins, were the Murdock MacEarca stock. The O'Devils and O'Donnellys in all likelihood sprang from Murdock MacErca. In descent from the northern clans Hugh Allen, King of Ireland, managed to obtain a series of victories over the descendants of Conall of Donegal. Hugh Allen, the King, had two brothers, Niall Frossach and Connor, whose descendants afterwards distinguished themselves. From Niall Frossach, by way of Hugh Finlay, were descended both the McLoughlins and O'Neills; the O'Neills derive their name from Niall Glundubh (Niall Black-Knee). These tribes provided great leadership potential to the tribes of the north. Kings were provided from Murdoch's line. From the other brother of Hugh Allen came a number of small clans whose combined power made up the kings of the north. It was the descendants of Connor, the Clan Connor, that gave rise to the fortunes of this clan. It was often called Connor Magh Ithe of the Fir Magh Itha (Men of Magh Itha). Magh Itha covers a fair part of the Irish countryside stretching south from Inish-Owen, later to be called the Laggan district in East Donegal. Connor had twelve sons, from one of which, Drugha, were descended the O'Cahans (O'Kanes). The O'Mullans were also descended from Connor. The McCloskeys were descended from one Blosky O'Cahan, and were later active in South Derry. This is mentioned in the Annals under the year 1196.

The hard resistance at Derry had been overcome. The Cianachta tribe, whose leading sept was the O'Connors of Glengiven in the Roe Valley, had held out here for many centuries. The Cianachta and the O'Connors were overthrown. Between AD 900 and AD 1000, according to Kelly's reckoning, the families of the Clan Connor vacated the occupied territory of Magh Itha. They eventually established themselves in the territory of the Foyle to the river Bann in County Londonderry. There are no records of the Cianachta having been attacked, but this we will deal with later. Where the process of the conquest ends, the various septs of Clan Connor had started to settle in the county. The Clan Dermot, and its chief family, O'Corrolan, south of the Faughan River, and the O'Cahans, O'Mullans and McCloskeys, stayed to settle all over the North Derry region.

The expansion of the Clan Owen took several centuries. Along with this, several other changes took place from which power might be exercised.

In ancient times the capital of Tir-Owen was Aileach near Londonderry. For many centuries the Kingdom of North-West Ulster attracted the two branches of the conquerors, the Clan Owen and the Clan Conall. The Clan Conall found it more difficult to expand because of its geographical situation. The balance of power shifted to the growing Clan Owen. There was a series of victories over Clan Conall by the Owen ri of King Hugh Allen and his kin. This resulted in the exclusion of the Clan Conall from the over-kingdom of the entire territory by the end of the tenth century. Clan Owen became the leading Ulster dynasty and Aileach now became the headquarters of the Clan Owen.

The ascendancy of the Clan Owen was not to last. Power swept further south deep into Tyrone (Tir-Owen), and a new capital was required. The central position of Tullyhog near Cookstown was chosen. James Hagan in his work *The Irish Law of Kingship* places this transfer of power to between 1035 and 1050. So then, as it is today, Aileach is a capital of the past, massive in earth and stone, but always regarded romantically by the lovers of this ancient seat. As the power of the Clan Owen expanded into Ulster, Aileach became a more and more a northern outpost of the clan. Other chieftains arose to power but not to the rank of Aileach. They were known as the Mulfoyle chiefs. A poem was written about the site:

> Worthy much of excellence is Mulfoyle
> Beloved King, distinguished, handsome
> Brilliant eyes beneath a very haughty head
> Yellow hair upon a fair shoulder.

Now Inishowen was lost to Clan Owen as a result of a succession of causes. Firstly there was the position of the Clan Binny, a big section of Clan Fergus and the royal clan descended from Muircherteach. This weakened the northern outpost and was followed by internal warring within the remaining Clan Owen over the fertile lands of Magh Ithe, lying to the south of Inishowen. The weakening of these clans gave an opportunity for the O'Doherty of Donegal to make a bid for absolute power. They were a powerful branch of the Conall peoples of Donegal. They had forced their way into Magh Ithe, and used this base for further expansion into Inishowen. Discontent in Donegal followed. The Owen families held the northern part of Inishowen and they were finally beaten in two famous battles. The first was a combined attack in 1117 by the forces of Clan Conall. Secondly there was the invasion from Scotland about a century later in which Trad O'Mulfoyle, lord of the remnants of the Clan Fergus of Inishowen, was slain, along with many of their people. So it was that the O'Dohertys and Clan Conall claimed themselves to be masters of Inishowen, the homeland of Clan Owen.

The clan was now operating as a force based in Ulster. The McLoughlins and the O'Neills ruled at the apex of the clan's power. At an earlier date the Kingship of the North-West had alternated between Clans Owen and Conall. When the kingship was in Owen's hands there was a competition for power between the McLoughlins and the O'Neills, both houses sometimes ruling at the same time. The McLoughlins now lapsed into obscurity, but the successors could not lie easy in their beds – if the old saying is true that 'uneasy lies the head that wears the crown'. Eventually the O'Neills shifted their power base from Tullyhog to Dungannon. They ruled now in the middle of County Tyrone. The main power bases around the O'Neills were those of the Clan Fergus, vigorous chieftains, 'victorious over foes on every hill'. They had once held territory as far north as Enagh Lough in County Londonderry; they were now dispersed in County Tyrone. Their lands lay around Tullyhog before their successors pitched camp at Dungannon. The O'Mellan sept had a large and well-defined territory which embraced Slieve Gullion in the north and Cookstown in the south. The extremity was known as Mellanaght. To the south of these lands lay the O'Hagan sept, who were at length transplanted to a region just north of the O'Mellans. The O'Quins' land probably lay to the south-west of the O'Mellans in the region of Lissan.

There were landowners in the other Owen families. There was the Clan Ferady, governed by McCawells, and settled around Clogher. To the north, the Clan Moen and its leading tribe, the O'Gormleys, settled to the east and north-east of Strabane. The O'Devlins settled in a region between the Clan Fergus lands and Lough Neagh. The O'Donnelly lived at Castle Caufield near Dungannon. The expansion of the sons of Owen now ended, for it brought the O'Neills to the pinnacle of their power over the clans and into modern times. The O'Donnells of Donegal had risen to power within the Clan Conall and had shaken off O'Neill power, and these people of the ruling Gaelic clans moved forward to meet the challenges of the new age.

# Chapter 3

## *At the Height of Power*

The O'Neill kingdom of course was nothing like a modern state with precise frontiers and defined power. There was a personal exercise of power that spread across as far afield as North-West Sligo, North Fermanagh, Armagh and Monaghan. The fatherland was Derry and Tyrone. This consisted of the Sperrin Mountains with their high ranges along the Derry/Tyrone border. The main power alternated between O'Neill in Tyrone and O'Cahan (O'Kane) in Derry. The O'Cahan had supported the O'Neills at Druim-dearg, where the Irish soldiers fought in linen tunics, with sword, spear and light axe against their enemies, who wore armour. Centuries later, O'Neill, Earl of Tyrone, had voiced his reliance on O'Cahan and his men saying that 'as long as he had O'Cahan and his country secure behind him, he cared little else for anything that they could do him'.

O'Cahan was the power behind O'Neill, and paid to O'Neill an annual tribute of twenty-one cows. They also paid the normal Irish services in peace and war. They enjoyed therefore a good deal of independence, electing their own chief by the law of tanistry. The choice of chieftain fell upon the best candidate by birth, and they ruled by age and worth, proclaiming themselves 'The O'Cahan'. This choice was confirmed by 'The O'Neill'. O'Cahan in the same way had a say in the inauguration of an O'Neill. O'Cahan was the chiefest of The O'Neill's uriaghts (vassals), and created him 'The O'Neill' by casting a shoe over his head, upon a hill in Tir-Owen (County Tyrone), a place always kept for inaugurations. The ceremony took place at Tullyhog and not at Dungannon, for Tullyhog was a very ancient seat of power. The ancient rath, two concentric ramparts of earth and stones, stands on a substantial and quietly sloping hill just beyond Tullyhog village. Today the site is adorned with beech and fir trees. In spring the banks are carpeted with violets, primroses and wood anemones. Rich grassland slopes down the hillside and cattle graze on the slopes that have borne the footprints of many famous Gaels. Opposite Tullyhog village there is an impressive view towards Cookstown and beyond. At Loughrig, near at hand, was the home of the Lindesays for 300 years. Here the first voices of Ulster youth ring out, learning the keeping of soil and stock. The countryside is dotted with prosperous farms, which lies quiet beneath the old rath where the O'Neill ruled over his subjects, and held the land that their ancestors had won.

Life and events have been put together by academics. They have looked to Armagh and the historical tracts, supplemented by information gained from the English state papers of the sixteenth century. It is possible to imagine the inauguration of a chief or king (ri) as performed in the Cinel Owen kingdom in post-Norman centuries. The new O'Neill was inaugurated by the several branches of the O'Neill line. The new king was conducted to the enclosure of Tullhog, near the present-day village of Tullyhog. Here stood the flagship of the ris – in actual fact a chair or a throne. O'Hagan was the chief elector of the O'Neill, in charge of the hereditary site where the ri was proclaimed. He along with the O'Mullan and O'Kane exercised their hereditary right in proclaiming the ri. O'Hagan escorted O'Neill to the inauguration stone. The king-designate was then given the rod by O'Kane, who was the senior sub-king of the Cinel Owen.

It was also the prerogative of O'Cahan to cast a shoe over the O'Neill's head – a custom that can be derived from the Bible: a symbolic act that indicated the assumption of rule over lands (Pss. 60.8 and 108.9). O'Hagan now had the honour of presiding over and reading the law. O'Mellan administered the oath on the Bell of Saint Patrick which was kept in a beautiful shrine. The united strength of the Clan Owen in Ulster was intertwined in the history of the clan which brought O'Neill to power.

The English had introduced into Ireland the policy of 'Surrender and Re-grant', whereby the Gaelic chieftain surrendered his land to the English monarchy. Conn Bacach, then the O'Neill, was first of all created Earl of Tyrone. However, there were many O'Neills of strong fibre, e.g. Shane O'Neill, who rejected all English titles and was faithful to the Gaelic system of inauguration. Shane was a handsome man and an uncompromising opponent of English rule in Ulster or anywhere else in Ireland. He said that the English government had cared little if he received a title. He said that his blood was of a higher nature than that of the invader. He said that he would not give in to anyone but the cousin of Kildare, for he was of the O'Neill's house. He said that "My ancestors were kings of Ulster, and all Ulster is mine and shall remain mine."

Britain was determined to impose the new law. Shane O'Neill and Red Hugh O'Neill loved the Gaelic system and their simple Gaelic life, and the name of O'Neill brought great prestige to Ulster. Shane was not boasting. Ulster was, however, the Black North, but for twelve centuries the Ulster descendants of the sons of Owen had risen to heights of power in the province. Chiefs or kings like Niall Glundubh, who was slain on the field of battle against the Norse at Dublin in 919, stood in the way of any permanent Norse settlement in Ulster. Tyrone, or Tir-Owen, remained substantially remote from later Norse invasions of Ulster. Tyrone was a central bastion. The Ard-Cianachta was the centre of O'Neill power, and O'Cahan power remained unsubdued. The Ulster that they ruled was an attractive land of fertile plains and colourful rivers. There were also many mountains, though not very high. There were the deep forests and bogs, where local power stood in the way of the invader. The proud hills of Tyrone were all part of the opening of the modern age, and the princes of the O'Neills had never been crushed by the British Crown.

The Sperrin Mountains were ruled by the O'Neills, and they had a lesser counterpart lying on either side of the range of hills that intrudes into County Londonderry and reaches Lough Foyle below the precipice of Benevenagh. From here on O'Cahan chieftains could survey the eastern Tyrone prospect. There were the proudly towering hills, finger dunes and shingle that cleft Lough Foyle and were common to Inishowen. The ancient Owen was now the stronghold of the O'Doherty. Taking a look inland, the greater areas stretched from Enagh and its castle, behind the common wood and hill of Loughermore. Beyond this lay the peaks of Dart and Sawel, their foothills golden in summer with arrays of whins. Dungiven Castle guarded the Glenshane Pass and the old priory, where for ages the O'Cahan chiefs had been buried. Further downstream was Limavady Castle, situated on a lofty rock near which a dog had leaped into the river in pursuit of a stag. It is preserved in memory as 'The Leap of the Dog'. Here there were peaceful valleys, rich in corn and cattle. There was also the salmon and trout of the sparkling streams. The red deer was hunted by the Gael as well as the great golden eagle. During winter the marches on the Lough side were a fowler's paradise, teeming with wild geese, ducks, plovers and swans.

A range of hills stretched back from Benevenagh through Knock anBaan and Cruick na huircle to Benbredagh and Carntogher. Benevengh was the land of the Magillans. Here the river Roe wended its way to the Atlantic. On the eastern sides of the range lay the little parish of Dunboe, so often a gateway to the heart of Ulster in the east. Here there were the famous castles of Coleraine and Castleroe. They were near Loughan Island, which divides the Bann. The McHenry O'Cahan held out across the Bann opposing the Scottish MacDonnells at a stream known as Garry's Flush, after Garry O'Cahan. The Norman McQuillands were lords of

Dunluce Castle, and had been in command beside the river Bann. Along the northern coast lay Dunseverick Castle, held by the O'Cahan family under the MacDonnells. The MacDonnells were a powerful clan and made a steady advance in acquiring more land. They hunted in the Glens of Antrim and in the Route or North Antrim. They ruled eastwards, meeting Clan Connor in the valley of the Bann. From O'Cahan's position it was possible to see the ships sailing into Lough Foyle. In an earlier age the Gaels would have seen the Vikings coming up the Foyle. The Normans came after them, building their castles along the coast and founding other ones as they penetrated Ulster with a view to a conquest. They founded castles in the valleys of the Bann and Roe. Shadows were now gathering, not only for the O'Cahans but also for the Ulster clans that were descended from Owen's favourite sons.

# Chapter 4

## *A Bid for Power*

Let us now look backwards in time, and see how the O'Cahans had attained and held their position. There are records of the lords of the Cianachta produced by the O'Cahan. The Irish Annals, most notably in the earlier period, records striking incidents rather than a connected historical account. In the Annals the richness of the Gaelic woodlands is described.

The O'Cahan now conquered the Cianachta. This took place between the invasions of the Vikings and that of the Normans. The Norse invasion had got under way by the ninth and tenth centuries. The Annals of Ulster record in AD 838 that there was great pillaging around Lough Neagh (Loch-Echach), and this helped to destroy Christian life in Ulster. The Vikings reached it as they rowed up the river Bann into the Antrim area; the Vikings had made a great impression on the north coast (or Fochla, as it was called). Another entry, under the year AD 865, shows that Aedh, son of Niall, plundered all the fortresses of the Vikings between Eogain and Dal Araide. They carried off their spoils of flocks and herds to his camp after battle. A victory was gained over the Vikings at Loch-Febhail (Lough Foyle), where many fighting men lost their heads to the sword and axe of the enemy. Dunseverick was captured by force – a great feat.

The first part of the tenth century was characterized by extensive activities by the Norsemen. The Clan Owen leader was slain by the Vikings. He was Muirchertach of the Leather Cloaks, and also Abbot of Coleraine. The mountains possessed much treasure, but the Annals of Ulster record under the year AD 944 that Donnell and Flaherty, sons of Muirchertach, killed the foreigners of Lough Neagh and destroyed their fleets. Ten years later Donnell took ships from the Bann Estuary and embarked on a raiding expedition that took him to Lough Neagh and Lough Erne.

The Norse had struck great terror into the life of the Ulster Gaels. But the Battle of Clontarf in 1014 marked the end of Norse rule, when the Gaels were led by the High-King Brian Boru.

The eleventh century was a period of expansion for the Clan Owen. At the beginning of the eleventh century, an important position in the north was held by the Clan Owen chief known as Flartery of the Pilgrim Staff, so called after he had made a pilgrimage to Rome. He was a great raider of the other Gaelic lands in which the pilgrim staff was replaced by a sword. By the middle of the eleventh century the men of Magh Ithe (the Clan Connor) rose to fame by raids upon the Oriella and the Clan Binny of Lough-Brochait, whose territory was supposed to have stretched from the western side of the river Bann, north of Lough Neagh.

The original territory of Clan Connor was Donegal, and it seemed to be the next move to conquer North Derry. They would cross the Foyle and progress eastwards. The Annals of Ulster record under the year 1076 that the defeat of Belat by Aedh Ua Mael-Sechlainn, and by the men of Magh Ithe upon the Cianachta, led to great suffering. Belat had disappeared from the history books as a place name – but it appears in the plantation map of Sir Thomas Phillips, covering the grocers' lands. Between the river Foyle and the river Faughan, the situation of the Clan Connor was settled. The Clan Dermort gave their name to the parish of Glendermott (or Clandermott). It is interesting to speculate what would have happened if the Clan Connor had pushed eastwards over the river Roe and the river Bann. However, some think that the advance was made along the valley of the Bann.

There were very definite signs of pressure by the Clan Owen upon the tribes to the west of Lough Neagh and the river Bann during this century, and it was a movement in which the men of Magh Ithe or Clan Connor could take a part. There were numerous tribes: the Ui Tuirtre lay to the west of the northern shores of Lough Neagh. There were many septs of the Clan Binny and Fir Li to the west of the Bann and the Cianachta in the valley of the Roe. These pressures are recorded in the Annals of Ulster. The men of Magh Ithe raided the southern Clan Binny septs. The movements of Clan Binny of Loch-Drochait are recorded under the year 1053. Also it is recorded that the King of Tullyhog was slain by Clan Binny; in 1081 they killed the chief of the Ui Tuirtre. On a later occasion, when the Clan Binny appears in the Annals, it was always the tribe known as Clan Binny of the Glen that was the farthest north. Clan Binny appears to have been a puppet state between the northern pressures from the Tullyhog chieftains and the Cianachta of North Derry. In earlier centuries the Annals of Ulster tell us that clashes took place between Clan Owen and the Cianachta. Under 1014 the chieftain of the Clan Owen was killed by his brother and the Cianachta of Glinne-Geinhun. It appears that the centre of power was moving eastwards during this century towards the Bann and Lough Neagh. The seat of the Owen kingdom had moved from Aileach in Donegal to Tullyhog in County Tyrone.

There was internal trouble amongst the Cianachta in the opening years of the twelfth century. In 1101, the chief of the Cianachta was killed by Connor Glinne-Geimhin. Three years later the O'Connor chieftain was killed by his own people. Finally in 1112 the chief of the Cianachta was killed by his brothers in the cemetery of Banagher.

Four years previously it was recorded that the chief of Fermanagh was killed by a sept living at Ardstraw and by the men of Creeve, near Coleraine. Trouble was afoot. In 1138 it was recorded that Raghnall, an impartial lord of Creeve, Cianachta and Fir Li was killed by the Ui-Eoghain of the valley. The valley people appear to be the Clan Binny. The O'Cahan slaughtering meant a restless and violent future that occupies a large place in Ulster's history for the next five and half centuries. This is the first mention of the O'Cahans in the Annals of Ulster. The centre of pressure seems to have shifted to Tullyhog, which was burnt in vengeance in 1011, and had its forces uplifted by the Ulidians a century earlier. Donnell McLoughlin, King of Clan Owen, was pressurizing the west and south from Tullyhog. Clan Connor and the O'Cahans were pressing north, their object to drive the tribes of Fir Li and Ui Tuirtre across the river Bann. The Clan Binny was subdued and now disappears from the Annals, while the O'Connors, once chiefs of the Cianachta, were forced to be small farmers in the district that they had formerly ruled.

The O'Cahans are seen thrusting against the Cianachta, the attack coming from the south up the Bann Valley and then across the mountains, but this can be disputed. There were two townlands named in the parish of Killelagh, which points to the original settlement of the O'Cahans or O'Kanes. Tammeymullan, north of Maghera, was occupied by an O'Mullan; both the O'Mullans and the O'Cahans were descended from Connor. The O'Cahans had risen to pre-eminence inside the Clan Connor, and their territory stretched down to Lough Neagh. In the mountainous areas between the Roe Valley and South Derry, there are a number of places which probably experienced struggles which had escaped mention in the Annals. Others have come down to us, but these do not correspond to townland names. In the parish of Rasharkin, the townland of Crushbracken is a place called Slaghttaggart, which means monument for the dead. These place names are associated with the O'Neill, Manus and Averty. The names were also affected by the Norse invasions. Manus or Magnus is a Norse name.

The O'Cahan were faithful benefactors of the Catholic Church, and an Augustine priory was founded at Dungiven in early times. These early connections with the Derry area seem to be at Creeve and in the expanse of hills that lie between the Bann and the Roe. It was an O'Cahan of the Creeve that dedicated the doorway of the refectory of the Black Church of Columba at Derry. However, it appears that the O'Cahan regretted the generosity to the church at a later date. The O'Cahan conquest of the Cianachta seems to have come from the Bann Valley and across the mountains. The bards sang their regret at the state of violence in the north. Darkness and silence surrounded Dungiven in its power and splendour in days long ago. Here stands the castle of O'Cahan and here lay the acres under his sway. Beyond the Moyola, the Bann and the Faughan, lay their chieftains. Here also rests the church at Dungiven where there were offerings for victory over the foe. Ireland's flag was unfolded to the free winds of heaven, and it marshalled its forces on the banks of the river Roe.

From 1138 the O'Cahans appear often in the Annals. Much mention is given to them between 1156 and 1178 and it records the internal feuds of the clans until the arrival of the Normans in 1169. The Annals show the O'Cahans taking part in tribal conflicts during the first half of the century, which followed their expansion into the districts of Creeve and Cianachta. By the third century the history of the north continued to influence the destiny of the clans until the arrival of John de Courcy and his knights, the Normans, in the County Down in 1177. He set out without royal leave to invade and conquer Ulster. He came from Somerset and he knew that Ulster was the most violent of the Irish provinces. He had been described as a tall, fair man of great strength and great daring, and the adventurers that he gathered about him were well sited for the coming task. De Courcy's first move was to capture the Gaelic kingdom of Ulidia in 1177, and from this moment Downpatrick was the capital of the Ulidia Norman knights. From here de Courcy turned north and he occupied half of County Antrim, where he came across Cumee O'Flynn, the chieftain of Hy Tuirtre and Fir Li. O'Flynn pursued a scorched earth policy and burned Armoy before de Courcy could arrive. De Courcy burned Coleraine and many churches, but he received a defeat by Cumee in the district of Fir Li. De Courcy was raiding some cattle when he was attacked in a narrow pass and barely escaped with eleven of his knights to his capital at Down.

The Irish in times of strife could never marshal themselves into a united front, and this helped de Courcy in his plans for the north. The Ulidians and the Ui Tuirtre bore the brunt of the Norman attack. Rory McDonlevy and Cumee O'Flynn had been his main opponents. They stood in the way of the Norman attack in the territories of the McLoughlins and the O'Cahans. In the Annals under the year 1181 it is recorded that Donnell McLoughlin had invaded Ulidia and defeated the Ulidians, Hy Tuitre and Fir Li. O'Cahan with the men of Magh Ithe and the Clan Binny of the Valley mustered an army and crossed the river Bann at Toome. They plundered all the territory of the Fir Li and Hy Tuitre and drove off many thousands of cows. Now Fir Li disappears from the Annals and the Clan Binny had disappeared from the Annals 150 years previously. The Normans killed Cumee O'Flynn, and Ui Tuirtre became a subordinate territory with an O'Flynn chief subject to the Normans.

The policy pursued by the McLoughlins and O'Cahans was thrown into relief by the happenings of the very next year. Donnell, the son of Hugh McLoughlin, marched with an army to Dunboe in the kingdom of Dalriada. Here they fought the English. The Clan Owen was defeated, and amongst the slain was Gilchrist O'Cahan. Dalriada is often pictured as being on the Antrim side of the river Bann. It is pointed out under the entry in the Annals of the Four Masters that there were records carried over from the earlier Annals of Ulster and the Annals of Kilroan. In early times the river Bann and the Bann Valley did not divide but tended to unite the Dal Riata. This seems to be true of the Normans' experience. Dalriada is likely to have expanded west across the Bann at an early time on the Derry side of the river.

The pursuit of tribal quarrels only helped to keep the Gaels in disunity. There were private quarrels. The Gaels were defeated in 1182, and this was to be repeated again. Under the year 1196 the Annals record that Murtough McLoughlin, said to be heir presumptive to the 'throne' of Ireland, and the destroyer of cities and castles of the English, was slain by Donough, son of Blosky O'Cahan, at the instigation of the Clan Owen. Blosky was the ancestor of the McCloskeys, who were later found as a sept in O'Cahan country. In 1197 the Normans were starting to settle in the Coleraine and North Antrim region, which was to exert great influence on the neighbouring O'Cahans. Under 1197 it is recorded that Sir John de Courcy and the English of Ulidia marched with an army to Eas Creeva and erected the castle of Kilsanton. He left Ratsel Pitun, together with a large force, at the castle, using it as a way to obtain territories and churches. Pitun later went on an excursion to the harbour of Derry and plundered the churches of Cluin-I, Enagh and Dergbruagh. But the Lord of Kinel-Owen and Kinel-Conall overcame the expedition of the northern Ui Neill, and a battle was fought between them on the strand of Faughanvale at which the English were slaughtered.

De Courcy followed this up by more expeditions to Derry and Inishowen and into Tyrone. De Courcy was at last ejected from Ulster in 1205. King John gave to Hugh de Lacy all the lands of the de Courcys which he could subject. De Lacy made his headquarters at Carrickfergus, where the great Norman castle dates from this early medieval period. The Ulster tribes fought the Normans as hard as they could. The Annals of Ulster record under the year 1206 that an army was led by the son of Hugh de Lacy with the English of Meath and Leinster to Tullyhog. They burned churches and corn, but did not obtain hostages nor pledges of submission from Hugh O'Neill on this occasion. An army was also led into Kienaghta, where they also burned churches and drove off numerous heads of cattle. Churches at this time were used for the storing of corn, making them a target for the conqueror.

King John expelled de Lacy in 1210, but he was later restored to his lands in 1226–27. During this interval great changes had taken place in the grant lands in the north and north-east of Ulster. They came under a Scots nobleman's influence: the Earl of Galloway was assigned on the King's behalf with 140 knights. They would extend their influence over the whole of north-east Ulster from the river Foyle to the Glens of Antrim. Ten knights on each side of the river Bann were exempted. The castle at Kilsanctan, however, remained in possession of the King. Under the year 1211 the records show that Thomas McUchtrig (the Earl of Athol) sailed with a fleet of seventy-six ships to Derry, and he plundered Inishowen. King John granted in the same year a part of Derry that belonged to the O'Neills. MacUchtry in 1214 started to plunder Derry, carrying off articles belonging to the churches at Derry and at Coleraine. In 1214 he strengthened his position at Coleraine by building a stone castle in the area. He found the materials to build the church by demolishing all the cemeteries and buildings in the town, except the church. The Scots noblemen received a gift off the King for Kilsabton and Coleraine Castles, with the knights facing each other on either side of the Bann. The raids on Ulster by the men of Galloway in Scotland were regularly followed by grants of land from the Crown. Grants were also made to Duncan of Carrick, and this marks the beginning of the long relationship between Galloway and north-east Ulster, which has continued into modern times.

The Ulster tribes were still in revolt, and it is doubtful that these grants of land from the Crown held any validity west of the river Bann. Farrell O'Cahan was killed in 1213. He had been chief of the Cianachta and Creeve, and had been killed in fighting against the English. The Ulster chiefs had still not been able to show a united front, and it is surprising to see that Farrell's successor led the O'Cahans to seize the house of McLoughlin's son. The prior of the Abbey Church of Derry, with Christian zeal, tried to make peace, but met his death. These grants to the Scots were restored by the de Lays in 1222. The son of Hugh de Lacy arrived in Ireland without the King's blessing, to obtain the assistance of Hugh

O'Neill, and set out with this end to fight the English not only in Ulster but in the rest of Ireland. One of their first actions was to march on Coleraine, where they demolished the castle, which had only recently been built. De Lacy, though restored to his lands in Ireland, was denied the lands of Alan and Thomas of Galloway. Shortly after this Coleraine Castle was rebuilt, but by whom, it is not known. The feud between the de Lacys and the Scots nobles was long-standing, and eventually the Scots estates in the north had disappeared. Some years later Patrick, son of Thomas of Galloway, was murdered. Walter Bisset and his nephew John were accused of the murder and were outlawed in Scotland. They fled to Ireland, where they were able to gain grants of land in County Antrim, previously held by nobility from Galloway. These grants almost certainly were granted by de Lacy, who, however, died in the same year, without male heirs. The Bissett territories were eventually granted to a girl who was the only heiress: Mairi Bisset married a MacDonnell of the Isles, and through her the MacDonnell took over Glenarm and the Glens of Antrim. They rose to a situation of great authority in the north.

The Clan Owen began to quarrel, and the Normans capitalized on their disunity. Norman power had been gradually gaining strength, and the Annals for the year 1238 show that the Lord Justice, with de Lacy, the Earl of Ulster, had got rid of McLoughlin from the chieftainship of the Clan Owen. The government of Tir-Owen was given to the son of O'Neill. The power struggle between McLoughlin and O'Neill led three years later to the battle of Cameirge, when the O'Neill with the company of the O'Donnells of Donegal defeated McLoughlin, who was killed. The site of the battle is unknown, but the traditional site for it is near Maghera. The Annals now state that there is a paucity of information about the early period. The Annals record that O'Kane, Lord of Kienaghta and Firnacreeva, was killed by Manus O'Kane after having led an expedition into his country as far as Antrim Dalriada. The O'Cahan were now in possession of Dunseverick Castle, the age of the plantation or colonization of Ulster. The lands governed by the O'Cahans of the Route are most probably the remnant of O'Cahan possessions across the Bann in pre-Norman times. Under the year 1171, Magnus McDunlevy's plundering into North Antrim was countered by an O'Cahan.

Under the year 1248, according to the Annals, the Lord Justice of Ireland led an army into Tir-Owen to combat O'Neill. A council was held and it was agreed that some English of Ireland at this time had ascendancy over the Gaels of the island. It would have been wise to make peace with O'Neill, and to give hostages. The English arrived at Coleraine, where they built a bridge across the river Bann. They also erected the castle of Drumtarcy and a dwelling at Drom. The castle was probably erected to defend the bridge, and was almost certainly on the far side of the Bann. They gave up a parish at Drumtarcy, which probably lay between Camus and Dunboe.

The peace that had been agreed did not last long, and the Clan Owen were intent upon driving off Norman power at the battle of Druim-dearg at Downpatrick. It was led by Brian O'Neill, and the Clan Owen fell in a noble defeat, in which the clans played a great part. The Irish did not take favourably to armour and went into battle in most attractive tunics, beautifully embroidered and dyed golden and saffron. The Normans of course were heavily armoured. The courage of the Gaels against the Normans in battle was not enough, for the Normans drove back the Gaels and defeated them with their armour. Brian O'Neill was killed and with him fifteen of the O'Cahan chiefs, showing the extent of the native effort and its dauntless quality.

Two poems relate Ulster's losses in this battle – one by MacNamee, the O'Neill bard, and another one by Fearghal Og-na-Bhaird, whose principal interest was the O'Cahans. MacNamee mentions the loss of Magnus O'Cahan as being the most pitiable after that of O'Neill. In the lament, the mouth of the river Roe is mentioned, and the six members of the O'Cahan clan mentioned are probably the heads of the septs. They also appear in Mac-na-Bhaird's poem. In the Annals of the Four Masters a Hugh O'Cahan is recorded as having fallen. In some respects Mac-na-Bhaird's lament is one of the great poems, but it strikes a more personal note. Magnus O'Cahan was probably educated by Mac-na-Bhaird's father, such was the Irish custom. The poet was his playmate and some years younger than him. Eahmarcach was Magnus's brother and was also fostered in the Mac-na-Bhaird home. The bonds between the two foster brothers were very close.

The value of the two poems lies not only in their literary quality, but also in that they are contemporary documents, and as such provide some insight into the history of the O'Cahans, as well as the political situation. A duel is recorded – the leading body of the O'Cahans remained in the field of battle until the next day, amongst the dead. Mac-na-Bhaird's poem refers to O'Cahan of Clooney, near Derry – as far away as Clooney! O'Cahan is called King of Formaeil, and the parish church of Dunboe is mentioned as well as the glen of Binny. The Formaeil mentioned were probably the Formaeil of Glenullin. The glen can be identified with Glenconkeyne. The O'Cahan, it is thought, replaced the Clan Binny in the glen and mountains in the approach to the valley of the river Roe.

The forces of Ulster and Connaught managed to gain a measure of unity, and fought the Battle of Down. This has been described as the most formidable Gaelic effort that the Normans in Ulster had to meet in the thirteenth century, and in time the O'Cahans played a great part. Brian O'Neill, and also Magnus O'Cahan and other chiefs fell in what is called Catha an Duin (the Battle of Down). The Battle of Down marks an epoch in Irish warfare and in Ulster history. The Normans remained unchallenged with their superior equipment until they were confronted by the similarly clad Gallowglasses, who had made their way across the province. From the thirteenth century Norman power became more and more entrenched in the north-east.

# Chapter 5

## *The Normans*

From the conclusion of the Battle of Down the Normans held a position of ascendancy in Northern and Eastern Ulster. This affected other spheres, for example land and cattle that belonged to the O'Neills and the O'Cahans. The whole area of Norman ascendancy was based at Coleraine; grants and inquiries are available for the period, which paint an exciting picture. In Hugh de Lacy's time the Earldom of Ulster had been ruled by seneschals for the reigning monarch. Henry de Mandeville was bailiff of Twescard or North Antrim. His accounts are available over the four terms ending 1 November 1262. Manors existed at Agherton, Portrush, Dunluce, Dunseverick, Bushmills, Armoy, Loughgiel and Mount Sandal. Henry de Mandeville held two carncotes of land at Drumtarsy. Agherton was confiscated after the Battle of Down from O'Haugham, and the land was granted to Sir Roger de Auturs, who had played a leading role in the Battle of Down. De Mandeville's account shows the progress of his position on his estates, with mills being lucrative as well as the Bann fisheries.

The Earldom of Ulster was recorded in 1264 in favour of Walter de Burgh, who died in 1271. He was succeeded by Richard, known as the Red Earl. During the ascendancy of the Red Earl (from 1270–80) William Fitz-Warin was appointed a seneschal of Ulster. He was succeeded by Henry de Mandeville, who was thrown out of his bailiwick in Twescard by Fitz-Warin. Now a long quarrel ensued between Fitz-Warin and the Mandevilles, and this has thrown some light on the position of the Ui Tuirtre and the O'Cahans. Fitz-Warin took out an inquisition in December 1277 in relation to the behaviour of Sir Henry de Mandeville, and the bailiffs were sent in before he could discuss the matter with him.

The jurors said that Magnus Ochaam was slain at Down against the King's peace and the Lord Edward. After his death Hugh Ochaam offered to Sir Henry five hundred cows (or land at Fernecren and Kenack), to hold off the Lord Edward. Sir Henry returned to take them but condemned Magnus as a traitor to the King and the Lord Edward. Twenty-seven English men and women were killed by the followers of Sir Henry. This was carried out by the Irish of Turtria by consent of Sir Henry. The Irish of Turtria burnt the land of Ocaynymery and Cachery, and twenty-two were killed by the consent Sir Henry. Sir Henry burnt Coleraine (Culrath) – another thirteen Englishmen were killed. This inquisition shows the competition of the chieftainships of the O'Cahan after the Battle of Down. Cooey O'Cahan, son of Magnus, fell in battle in trying to obtain land. Perhaps Ocaynymery is synonomous for Drumsumery, known as Dunseverick Castle. It was the residence of this branch of the O'Cahans at the plantation/colonization of Ulster, and they seem to have remained in the Barony of Carey. Cooey O'Cahan in the Clan Ui Tuitre took the Mandeville way of action in the area.

Henry de Mandeville did not take these jurors' decisions about the bailiwick of Twescard lying down. In a letter from the Mayor and Community of Carrickfergus he stated that Hugh O'Neill, King of Clan Owen, and Cooey O'Cahan, King of Keenaught, at the prompting of the de Mandevilles, had high-handedly entered upon the King's land, burning, murdering and robbing. William Fitz-Warin, seneschal of Ulster, arrested those Englishmen for debts due to the King. They burned five towns and two thousand bales of wheat, and three mills belonging to him, depriving him of an annual rent of fifty-seven marks. They favoured the King's English subjects, saying that they would work the land, but they were confined by the policies of the seneschal, Hugh Bisset, and his friends. Many Irish chiefs, including O'Flynn, wrote to the King at the same time, capitalizing on the help that the seneschal had given them during the process of the attack. The de Mandevilles are said to have been instrumental in the burning of the clans. They are said to have burned William Fitz-Warin's manor of Croosscarnadry and five of his surrounding towns, totalling damage of £300.

For the fifty-year period that had elapsed from 1264 the de Burgh interests were of prime importance in the north and east of Ulster. A deed of the year 1269 records a debt of 3,500 cows, to be paid to de Burgh, Earl of Ulster, by O'Neill, King of Cinel Owen. Cooey O'Cahan may have been dispossessed following his part in the raid into North Antrim in 1273. Alternatively another O'Cahan was recognized as chief by the Normans. This appears in a deed of 1277 by which Dermort O'Cahan, King of Fir na Craibhe granted to Richard de Burgh the land of Glen Okenkahil, which he held of the Earl of Ulster, paying to him a fee. The place name has not been identified, but it seems to have lain between the O'Cahans and the O'Neills. Richard de Burgh granted it to

Henry O'Neill in 1312–3. Cooey O'Cahan kept it to himself, for it appears at the inquisition of 1282 regarding damage done by the Earl of Ulster and his men against Fitz-Warin in the lands of the latter in the north. It was also said that the de Mandeville, Cooey O'Cahan and the Gaelic chiefs had taken from Fitz-Warin 1,000 oxen and cows, 2,000 two-year-old hogs and goats and 1,000 horses and carthorses.

It had been conjectured that the Norman manor of Roe came into existence around the time of the surrender of Glen Okenkahil. He said that Angus Oge MacDonnell of the Isles, who had married Angus, a daughter of Cooey O'Cahan, was said to have received with her a dowry of seven score men. This included the Munros, so called because they came from Roe Water, their names being formerly O'Mullan, etc. But there does not appear to be a likely origin for the name Munro. It has been suggested that the dowry may well have been true for there was an exodus from the Roe Valley, which may have corresponded with the erection of a Norman manor there. Agnus outlived her husband, and returned to Ireland, where she may have remarried. John Mor MacDonnell of the Isles married her grandson, so the MacDonnells succeeded to the Glens of Antrim.

The records show that before the end of the century there was some evidence of Norman interest in the western side of the river Bann, and this encroached upon O'Cahan territory. The de Sandal family were active in the Portrush–Coleraine area, and it is said that they gave their name to Mount Sandal. William de Sandal and Thomas his son, were granted Lishcillin by the Abbot of Clerefonte, which had been the Cistercian monastery founded by the O'Cahans at the end of the twelfth century or in the early thirteenth century. Dunba (Dunboe) and Donathy are mentioned as churches. Donathy church is mentioned in the composition made by the Bishop of Connor, regarding the union of the churches of Donathy and Moydore. These churches appear to be in different dioceses. Donathy may be the church of Slut Donathy or Sillocht Donaghy. The two territories of Slut Donaghy and Slut Doneghy make up a border with the Aghadowey River, giving Slut Donaghy some other parishes. These included the parishes of Desertoghill, Errigal and part of Aghadowey Parish he assigned to Slut Gorry. Gorry may have stretched across the river Bann. There was a stream called Gorry's Flush and this may have been the boundary of Slut Gorry. Other lands recorded are Dasding and Drumdarach.

1279 is an important date – the Normans were now covering land well west of the river Bann and into the Roe Valley. At the turn of that year a marriage was arranged between Egidia, the Red Earl of Ulster's sister, and James, the Steward of Scotland. In the same year the King confirmed an act by which the Earl granted to James and Egidia their own castle at Roe and the lands belonging to it. The entire lordship as far as services and rents were concerned of the English enfeoffed by the Earl in Keenaught belonged to the Roe Valley on the east side of the river Roe. There was an island in the river near the castle and all the Earl's lands of Rennard comprised all farmers and feoffees, as well as land within and without the manor.

By the time of this charter the manor had been well established. It was in the O'Cahan land of Keenaught that Roe Castle may be the famous castle mentioned at the Dog Leap. The records do not record any island in the river at this point, and the castle is more likely to have been on the lower reaches of the Roe, where islands are clearly visible in the plantation period. The castle is perhaps more likely to have been situated near the mouth of the river from the point of view of protection by the strategic position of Lough Foyle. It is likely that the manor stretched west up the river. It has been recorded that Edmund de Burgo was Rector of Roe Priory in 1308. The church of Roe was valued as far as ecclesiastical taxation was concerned at the high figure of £20, and it may have also included the parish of Drumachose, and also those of Tamlaght-Finlagan, Balteagh and Agnanloo.

The Normans were now part of the everyday scene in Ulster, taking part in the fighting between the clans. In 1303 there was a protracted quarrel with the O'Donnells of Donegal, in which a lot of the countryside was ravaged. There were also a number of O'Donnells killed, but also many important Norman figures, including Adan Sandal. The chief of Fir-na-creeve and Kienaghta, Donn O'Cahan, was also slain. The presence of the Normans was now growing even more formidable. The Red Earl of Ulster had obtained an important foothold in Inishowen, and in 1315 he built the impressive fortress of Northburgh or Greencastle on a road which rises at the entrance of Lough Foyle, just opposite Magilligan Point. With the Roe on the opposite bank, it commanded the approaches to the Lough. In the same year the Red Earl obtained permission from the Bishop of Derry to build a parochial church at Northburgh.

However, over the next few years cracks appeared in the Norman hegemony. The Red Earl was growing old, but he was also an autocrat. His son John, who would have succeeded him, died in 1313. At this time Robert Bruce, who had been forced to take refuge on Rathlin Island, made a bid to free Scotland from the Norman yoke. In 1314, King Edward II wrote a letter to the Gaelic chiefs telling them to assemble themselves under de Burgo for service against the Scots. Amongst the names appearing was that of 'Dermod O'Kane', leader of the Irish of Fir-na-Cracbh, who had precedence over Donald O'Neills of Tyrone.

Bannockburn was Bruce's personal victory, and he now turned his attention to the Gaels of Ulster and Ireland, the raw material of an anti-English combination. Edward Bruce now landed at Larne Harbour in May 1315, with an army of 6,000 Scots veterans. He was joined by Robert Bisset of the Glens of Antrim, and by Donal O'Neill, son of Brian catha an duin. The most colourful of Bruce's activities is perhaps given in the Book of Clonmacnoise. According to it Edward Bruce and his army, in league with O'Neill and other Ulstermen, had journeyed towards Coleraine, and they broke the bridge there in order to prevent the Red Earl crossing over the river Bann. The Red Earl followed closely behind until he came to the river. From Coleraine he marched through all of Ulster, spoiling and destroying. Towns were ransacked. Places were burnt to mere ashes, churches were reduced to bare stone. There was some shooting of arrows on both sides of the river. The Red Earl therefore had confronted Bruce's army across the Bann. But Bruce was not to be beaten. He followed the Red Earl and defeated him at the Battle of Connor, near Ballymena. King Robert Bruce came over to Ulster to assist his brother in the autumn of 1316, but withdrew in 1318. Edward was defeated at Faughart, near Dundalk in 1318; he was also slain in battle. So the Scots invasion of the north came to an end, and its effects were to last for a long time, and also to be remembered.

Devastation followed the Bruce wars, particularly in Ulster. There was also disease amongst the cattle for three years, then an epidemic of smallpox followed by flu. There was also a great dearth of corn in 1328, 1330 and 1331. The Red Earl did not live to see the worst of the famine. He had been humiliated by defeat and there were questions about his loyalty. He had been imprisoned in Dublin Castle because his daughter was married to Robert the Bruce. He now retired to a monastery, where he died in 1316. After his death the worst of conditions prevailed. It was said that the tenth part of the King's land in Ulster was settled. There were subtenants and powerful landlords. The Norman forces were devastated, and their tenants were reluctant to return. Some of those lands were probably recognized by the northern clans, but much of the remainder lay derelict. It was suggested that a plantation/colony of Welsh and English settlers, to the number of 3,000 men would find enough wasteland over which the landlords power did not stretch.

The Red Earl of Ulster was succeeded by his guardian, William the Brown Earl, who was no match for the Red Earl. The Brown Earl was murdered near Belfast in 1333, leaving only an infant daughter. A look at his estates is interesting for the insight they give into the manor of Roe. The Brown Earl had manors at Northburgh in Inishowen, Roe, Keenaught and Camus, but these were laid to waste. The Roe estates comprised thirty-four carucates held by the tenants for several years, and each carucate was worth 26/8. These lands lay untilled because of the unsettled conditions in Ulster. Seventeen carucates had been in the hands of freeholders, who worked the mill of 'Le Roo', but there were also derelict mills. Those which were not derelict were a great source of profit, for the tenants were bound by their agreements with their landlords. There were two watermills in the Roe Manor, which had been worth twenty-eighty crannochs of flour at 2/- per crannoch. The profit was nil in 1333, and the same obtained at Drumtarsy, Loganstun and Dundoon.

Rory O'Cahan, King of the Gaels at Ferneerewe, was said to have held his military service from the Brown Earl. This system replaced another type of tenure, which demanded a yearly rate of cows from the Gaels and their clans. How far each system succeeded is open to question. This Rory O'Cahan was probably the Rory O'Cahan, Lord of Creeve and Ard Keanaghta, who died in 1349 according the the Annals of the Four Masters. The word 'An' seems to have been a mistake. If the Norman forces reached the manor of Roe, it may well be a correct description of the O'Cahan position in Keenaught at the time.

Now all of Norman rule in Ulster was fast disappearing, leaving behind only the great motes such as Kilcranny, Coleraine and Mount Sandal, and places designated as granges, such as the grange at Kildollagh. The word 'grange' is the old French for barn, and such names denote former Norman rule. A new system was now arising in the ashes of Norman power. The families that remained had to be ever vigilant of Gaelic uprising, which threatened the civilized Normans. They would have to keep their lands by use of the sword. The de Burghs became Burkes, the de Mandevilles became O'Quillans. In 1357 the area of North Antrim was called McQuillan territory. Lionel, Duke of Clarence, who had been married to the Brown Earl's only daughter and heiress, was named ruler of many lands in Ulster. She came to Ireland in 1361, finding the Earl of Ulster. The annalists record under 1474 that Niall O'Neill delivered a defeat on the foreigners, where fell the Knight of the Rock (Carrickfergus), also the de Burgh and William of Baile-dalat. O'Cahan was now claiming to rule in Ulster in accordance with his wishes and not in accordance with the English Crown.

# Chapter 6

## *The Fighting Clans*

Coleraine was easily accessible by sea, and it was one of the remaining enclosures of Norman power in Ulster. The Duke of Clarence tried to recover some of his wife's estates. In 1639 Coulrath (Coleraine) and Drumtarsy were numbered among his prize possessions. The Annals record that in 1376 Cooey O'Cahan was taken prisoner by the English at Coleraine and was sent to Carrickfergus in fetters. Carrickfergus was chosen because it was considered safer, for it was farthest away from O'Cahan territories. An attack was made by the O'Cahans on the English, but the Normans had still enough military strength in the area to seriously defend them. Drumtarsy Castle was still in existence, and in 1382 the Treasurer of Ulster was ordered to repair it and also to repair the bridge.

Cooey O'Cahan died in 1385 after either escaping or being released from captivity. His death came when he was at the height of his power. Tradition has identified him as the Cooey-na-Gall whose tomb is in the old priory of the Augustinian order which O'Cahan founded in the seventeenth century, on the site of an earlier Gaelic monastery. Today the walls of the chancel and the side walls of the nave are still in good condition. Within the ruin is the altar tomb of O'Cahan. He is represented by an almost lifelike figure of a man in armour, one hand resting on his sword. On the front and sides of the altar are six sculptured figures of O'Cahan's gallowglasses, clad in chain mail. The tomb has earned a reputation as being the most famous monument of the late Ulster Middle Ages.

Mystery surrounds the Cooey who died in 1385, whose name is on the famous altar tomb. Some authorities think that the linking of the tomb with the earlier Cooey, who succeeded Magnus an Duin, also took part in the quarrels between the Mandevilles and Sir William Fitzwarin. It has been argued that the canopy of the tomb is that of a later date than the effigy. The tomb bears a resemblance to the one in the abbey church of Roscommon, which has been ascribed to King Felim O'Connor, who died in 1265. The Gaels tried to follow the foreigners. The earlier Cooey-na-Gall of tradition can be connected back to the Scots of the Isles.

There has been much confusion between the two Cooeys. The Cooey who died in 1385 had a daughter – Finola or Finvola – who outlived him. The earlier Cooey's daughter has been mentioned not only as Angus, but also as Margaret and Hannah. Her correct name was almost certainly Agnes. A Chancery roll of 1338 gives a safe conduct to Agnes, mother of John of the Isles, protecting her as she crossed the sea to Ireland. There is a famous poem about the O'Cahan girl, who married a Scot, and when she died her body was brought back to Dungiven for burial. Granie Roe, of the O'Cahans, mourned her death. This girl is called Finvola, but many of the features look back to an earlier Agnes, wife of MacDonnell. The family had gone on to say:

> In the lands of the O'Cahans where bleak mountains rise,
> O'er whose brown ridgy tops now the dusky cloud flies,
> Deep sunk in a valley a wild flower did grow,
> And her name was Finvola, the gem of the Roe.

The burial inscriptions in front of the tomb of Cooey were reserved solely for the immediate descendants of the chief branch of the O'Cahans. The last of the family name to have been buried here was Bridget Doherty, who for years had been a wandering mendicant. Her ancestry could be traced back to the famous Cooey. The burial grounds were well guarded, and to be buried there was a great privilege. The honour that was conceded to Bridget would not have been granted to any others of the name, regardless of their wealth or standing, or who had hereditary claim to the honour.

Officers also were shown a dagger that was said to be connected with Cooey. The dagger was part of the Saxon's sword, found in the valley of Strangemore after a battle between the Saxon and Cooey-na-Gall. It is thought that it was preserved by a sept of the O'Cahan, and to have been fashioned into a weapon of defence when they were called to chase the Tory hunters or outlaws.

A small bit about Cooey's family is known. Finola and Cathal the Black outlived him. He was succeeded in power by Manus, who died in 1403, and Dermot who died in 1428. Primate Colton made a visitation of the diocese of Derry in 1397, and he came to the village of Dermot O'Cahan. Dermot's village was probably at Enagh Lough, which was an O'Cahan stronghold in the centuries to come. A matrimonial case was brought before the Primate by the chieftain Magnus (or Manus).

A woman called Una O'Connor appeared and she stated that she was the wife of Manus O'Cahan, head of his clan or nation, and had been dismissed by him without proclamation by the Church. She was replaced by another woman. Manus O'Cahan was summoned to appear, and when he did he was confronted by the charge that he had been married to Una O'Connor, had children by her and had then set her aside. Manus asked for time before he stated his point of view, and he denied that he was ever married to Una. Una was asked to produce witnesses. She called upon Donald O'Cahan and Master Simon O'Fenaghty, Canon of Derry Cathedral Church. The case was put off to the next day at Banagher, but it does not appear later in the visitation records. It is likely that a settlement was reached out of court. The townland of Killunaght in Banagher Parish was recorded in the OS Memoirs with the death of Owen O'Kane. O'Connor was the family name for the clan who had settled in the Roe Valley before its conquest by the O'Cahans.

The O'Cahans enjoyed considerable power in the first part of the fifteenth century. Anglo-Norman power was coming to an end. Feuds between the clans were now not so frequent as at a later date. Dermot Cooey's son died in 1428, and he was remembered as a man of great triumph and honours. Perhaps the most serious side of the business was the rainy Irish weather. In 1421 the Annalists also record that there was very hot weather in the summer, and that there were harvests of numerous nuts. For years later the weather was inclement from November to May. This caused great hardship for the cattle, and a loss of opportunity for tillage, resulting in death and shortages of food. Sometimes the food shortage was due to deliberate destruction of crops. In the Route, open and flat, McQuillan lacked mountain pasture and forest cover, and was often the victim of neighbouring tribes. In 1431 the O'Neill spent six weeks in North Antrim, destroying crops and burning villages. O'Neill himself was slain in O'Cahan country, and had to ward off attack from O'Donnell and Aibne, son of Dermot O'Cahan. They led their assault upon a house in which O'Neill was staying. Having attacked the house, they killed O'Neill and some of his people. The O'Neills, for some reason, did not retaliate. The Annals now tell us that the first serious conflict between the O'Cahans and the McQuillans took place. McQuillan, with O'Neill's help, routed O'Cahan with thirty-two of his people slain. The initial attack was followed up by more destruction. O'Cahan killed a son of a McQuillan chief. The McQuillans now raided the lands of Aibhe O'Cahan. However, these tribal conflicts were on a small scale, as shown by the number of tribesmen killed in the first encounter, even though they were on the losing side. The feuds of the O'Cahans and McQuillans were protracted, and it must have weakened the tribes when any attack from an external source took place.

The sons of Dermot O'Cahan seem to have taken a leading role in the affairs of Ulster in the first half of the century. Tradition has given Dermot twelve sons. McSperran, in his Irish legend of O'Donnell, gives their names: Cooey, ancestor of O'Cahan of Limavady, Dermot Turlagh, Shane Donall, Mortagh, Donough, Niall, Owen, Toal, Evenney and Patrick. He sites their residence as near the abbey of Dooneven (Dungiven). O'Cahan's Brook at the foot of Benbraddagh is also mentioned, as are Limavady; Swatteragh; Glenkeen, near Garvagh; Flanders, below Dooneven; Castle Roe (Castleroe), near Coleraine; Enagh, Ballyshesky, near Beechhill; Clanermott; Coolnamuuen; and Tiergolin. Cooey's name is best known, and Donnell and Aibne (Evenney) are mentioned in the Annals of the Four Masters. This list does not site Henry, who was the ancestor of the McHenrys of the Loughan. It does not mention Philip, from whom there is a record in the OS Memoirs, tracing events up to plantation times.

In the OS Memoirs of Drumachose Parish is recorded a castle being built upon the site, i.e. Killane, said to have belonged to the O'Cahans. It is also said that it gave its name to the Castle River and Castle Bridge. A deed of 1768 shows Henry O'Cahan of Cahan's Brooke active in the parish of Dungiven, and his daughter Margaret is recorded as having married Andrew Patterson of Maghera. Cooey plays an important role in the O'Cahan story. O'Cahan was never a chief himself, but his offspring fill the role of chieftain for the two centuries that followed the death of Dermot. Dermot was succeeded by Godfrey, his grandson, who died in 1433. Manus held the chieftainship for thirty-five years. As far as the records are concerned the key events took place at the beginning and at the close of the period. His succession is recorded in the Annals of Ulster, a year of great frost. The frost started nine weeks before Christmas and lasted seven weeks after Christmas. The lakes were like ice but herds of cattle, horses and people were able to move about freely. There were great losses in bird life a year before Manus died, and in 1468 O'Neill raided O'Cahan country. In the genealogies Manus has gone down as the man that constructed the Finnchuisg, leaving historians to wonder what this meant.

Rory II succeeded Manus, his son. Four years after his succession he was killed by the McQuillans of the Route, and so the ancient troubles between the two clans re-emerged. Vengeance would be encountered by O'Cahans, and a force would move into North Antrim in order to take lives. In the battle to follow Godfrey O'Cahan was killed with a single cast of a javelin by Rory McQuillan. The next day the McQuillans were defeated and their chief killed. Rory was now made chief of the Route, and crossed the mouth of the river Bann for peace discussions that had been arranged by the O'Cahans. He was crossing the Bann in a small boat, and here he was put to death by a party of the O'Cahans. His body was thrown into the Bann.

The chieftaincy of the O'Cahans now passed from Rory, who had just been murdered, to his second cousin, Sean, son of Aibhne. The chief of a clan was not automatically succeeded by the chief's son, but by the person best qualified militarily to take charge of the tribal lands. When the office passed from father to son for three generations, there was jealousy when the children of the next generation were passed over. With the arrival of the plantation period the position of the chief became important.

Sean O'Cahan was selected at a difficult time for the tribe, for in 1489 his son was captured by Conn O'Neill. O'Neill devastated O'Cahan territory. The next summer Sean O'Neill was captured by a Scots vessel from Inveraray. However, he was released in the following year, and showed his capacity for decisive action by returning stolen cattle from the son of Manus O'Cahan before anyone in the territory knew what was going on. Also a new O'Neill was proclaimed. The shadow of coming trouble cast gloom across the land. O'Cahan power was now on the wane and in the next century this became apparent during Sean's period of rule. The first serious trouble came in 1492. The two sons of Sean, Godfrey and John Galldan, were slain by Walter McQuillan at the instigation of their uncle, Thomas O'Cahan. In the summer of 1495 many raids took place on the O'Cahan territory by the McQuillan.

Events beyond his control typified the later years of Sean. In 1496 the Annals of Ulster record most inclement weather. Husbandry was affected and there were great losses of cattle, particularly in Fermanagh. There was a serious famine throughout all of Ireland; many died. Bad weather marked the beginning of the sixteenth century, with the loss of cattle and crops. The O'Cahans were now restless in power, rather like the weather. Family ties and relations with the Church were in a stable condition. Thomas had two nephews, Donough and Donnell, who were the sons of the former chief, Sean. They made a formidable trio. Donnell was educated in the Church and was nicknamed 'The Cleric'. He was fluent in Latin, but his attitude was anything but clerical. In 1503 he wounded his brother, Richard, but this was not an unusual event in tribal affairs, since only those that were physically fit could become chief, and potential rivals were sometimes got rid of in this way. In 1506 Donough killed his nephew, Manus, son of Brian the Fair. In the same year the O'Cahans crossed the river Bann with the help of this trio, killing McQuillan, and they returned to base with a great deal of cattle and horses.

The family that descended from Manus had enjoyed a long period in the chieftainship until his death in 1468. Donough O'Cahan was hanged, and he had been abbot of the Moscosquin monastery; in 1515 he himself was maimed and killed. Some years later the descendants of Manus O'Cahan killed Godfrey, son of Thomas the chief. There was jealousy between the two families – a jealousy that surrounded the chieftainship. Thomas now grew old, and the two contenders for the title were his nephews, Donnell the Cleric and Donough, who pursued policies of violence, in the same manner that they came to power. In 1513 Donnell the Cleric hanged O'Donnell, who had been held in Coleraine Castle, and he demolished it. The reason for the hanging was that O'Donnell the Cleric had violated a guarantee he had given. O'Donnell had lived at Coleraine, and is described as having come from there. Donough took his Uncle Thomas prisoner some time before his uncle had died in 1521. He was forcibly taken from his lordship.

There were now serious claims for the chieftainship over the next five years. In 1552 Donnell the Cleric, a man of great hospitality, was killed by the men of the Route in North Antrim. Now Donough died – 'the best patron of his own tribe in his time'. He was friend of both the learned and distressed. Donnell the Cleric also died. Now two lords were proclaimed in opposition to one another. One was Godfrey, son of Godrey and grandson of Sean, and the other was John, son of Thomas. John was a violent fellow and was supported by the people of the Route and by the O'Dohertys. The battle over the leadership went on during 1524 and many prominent O'Cahans were put to death. In 1525 John, son of Thomas, was killed on the night of the Lammas Fair by three of his own clan in which a leader was Rory of the Route. In 1526 the other contender was killed by an O'Neill. This left the heir to the chieftainship open; and Godfrey, son of Donough, was the obvious heir. He went on a raid in January into Glenconkeyne where he died of the cold weather, and his body was found later without a mark upon it. Manus, his brother, now succeeded as chief, after feuds that had torn the clan to pieces.

The account of the O'Cahan dispute with the McCloskeys has been recorded by the Church. It said that the O'Cahans were always fighting themselves and the enemy. The McCloskeys, for their favours under the O'Cahan, held a lot of lands lying west of the Roe, and having disputed with the Clan O'Mullan. They sent two lords forward to hunt towards Largywood, where O'Mullan drowned both of them in the river Roe. These terrible events were heard of as evening drew on. The flower of their young manhood were drawn away, again on another warlike expedition. Next morning, those who could arm themselves sent out another warlike expedition to meet their enemies. The encounter took place at Ballyclose in the suburbs of Newtownlimivady. It was a fierce and bloody battle, but the O'Cahans were eventually defeated, and all those who fell had their ears cut off. Their friends swore an oath that the O'Mullans heads should roll as a penalty for the murder. This, however, was not easily obtained but was the cause of further trouble at a town since called Derryland. In the cutting off of the heads, the person who was appointed to collect the insurgents together cast away the heads privately, but still the number required was insufficient. If a chieftain's head was given to him, and having thrown it away, his own head was answerable in its place. The heads were buried on the hill above mentioned, in sight of the castle window. It was hereafter called Knock-na-Ginn, or the Hill of the Heads.

The foregoing story is probably just a story, but the tradition is perhaps based on facts. The Ordnance Survey Department was shown the hill or tumulus of Knock-na-Ginn near Dungiven and were told the same story – that they were made to pay for the years lost at Ballyclare (the Town of the Ears). A pool in the river Roe was named O'Mullan's pool, referring to the connection with the fort of balliboes in the parish of Magilligan. Perhaps this pool is connected with tradition.

McSparran tells another story, that the last O'Cahan chief to live in the castle at Kane's Rock had arbitrary demands in relation to every newly married bride. He was almost killed by the O'Mullans near the village of Garvagh. This place was also chosen for another branch of the family. On the first market day at Dungiven, he rounded up a number of O'Mullans, and hanged them in vengeance for what had been done to him. McSparran recorded that he saw some labourers digging by the roadside, and that they had some skills. Here he was probably buried at the foot of the gallon, which was erected in sight of the castle windows. The gallon hill is named Ardgarvin. The Ordnance Survey Department was told that there was a small hill called Gallows Hill, east of the river Roe in the townland of Limivady. Here the last chief erected a gallows to punish those that believed that before long O'Cahan would be without a horse, and the hill without a fair.

The main feature of the age was the feuds between Manus O'Cahan and the McQuillans. The first incident took place in 1532, when the Annals record the death of McQuillan. He was slain in the church of Dunboe by the son of Rory of the Route and the son of Donnell the Cleric. Four years passed, and O'Cahan made a raid on McQuillan, who mustered his forces and obtained the help of the Scots, and lay in ambush for O'Cahan; he returned with his spoils. O'Cahan lost the fight and the booty, and McQuillan started to burn O'Cahan's house.

In 1542 another assault took place against the McQuillans by the

O'Donnells and O'Cahans. They marched to the river Bann and crossed despite opposition, and divided their forces into two detachments, one part lying east of Knocklayd, and another up the Bann. The third force was concentrated under O'Donnell and O'Cahan. Many heads of cattle were taken, some were driven away alive, whilst O'Donnell ordered that the cattle which could not be driven off should be attacked, killed or have their bones broken. In answer to this a raid was made by the McQuillans and the Scots, who entered O'Cahan territory and drove off cattle. Manus O'Cahan, together with the McQuillans and MacDonnells, was defeated, and a great number of their army were drowned while crossing the Bann. The troubles were recorded in the state papers. The Lord Deputy of Ireland and his council informed King Henry VIII that in 1542 the Gaels had submitted to His Majesty. But the O'Cahans rebelled with the aid of the Scots gallowglasses. A number of horse and foot were sent to the Route to aid McQuillan and also for the O'Cahans, who had never shown obedience to the King.

John Traver was Master of the Ordnance and warden of Coleraine Castle in 1542. The Annals record that McQuillan, having sought the help of the English, made another attack against O'Cahan, and they took O'Cahan's castle at Limivady. They put to death all the warriors in the town. McQuillan departed with his life and was victorious on this occasion. At the close of 1542 Manus O'Cahan made his submission to the King and signed an indenture of peace, but the peace was not to prove long-standing. In 1544 O'Donnell raided the Route and captured Loughan Island in the river Bann. Here McQuillan had a wooden castle, and also Ballylough Castle. The island was given to the O'Cahans by O'Donnell, but they were not due to have possession of it for very long, and the MacDonnells of Antrim rode against Loughan Castle, and seized it from O'Cahan's warders, and burned Brian, son of Donough O'Cahan, together with their weapons. It is against this feuding background that took place between the O'Donnells and O'Cahans on one side and the McQuillans on the other that the grand battle took place near Drumachose old church. Some remains were discovered many years later when building the mail coach road between Limivady and Coleraine. There was also a nearby graveyard that was excavated and some skulls were found of those who had fallen in battle. Another pit of bones was uncovered in Gortmore, north of Drumachose old church, by labourers who were making a ditch.

Now enters a love story featuring Laura O'Donnell, with, however, a tragic end. Laura was in love with Finn McQuillan when their representative class started a feud. She awaited the result of the battle on the Limivady side of the church, still called Crossmadonnell. Finn was killed in the feud and Laura is said to have died at the same time. They were buried in the townland of Cahery, beside the banks of a little river, the Curly. A cairn is raised over them called Cairn a Finn.

Manus O'Cahan was killed in 1548 taking part in a feud with the O'Donnells along the banks of the river Finn, near Ballybofey. Both sides were weakened as a result of the quarrel, and in 1553 O'Cahan land is described as having been wasted. English power in the region had increased since the time of Donnell the Cleric. A journey was now undertaken by the Earl of Sussex in 1556. On 14 July he came to the river Bann, where boats met him. A camp was set up by the river called Kocksendall, and there was a monastery in the region called Collrahan (Coleraine). Beneath the hill there is a castle called Castan Louhan, belonging at one time to James McHenry in the Route (the Roet). In the monastery were buried the ancestors of McGillan. Following this came the bishop's house which boasted a castle and a church joined together in one place called Ballymoney.

These were the years of the notorious Shane O'Neill Shane the Proud, as he has been called. He was undisputed master of Ulster until 1567. The Statute of 1567 attainting O'Neill also attainted O'Cahan, the O'Cahan lands being forfeited to the Crown. But no effort seems to have been made to uphold the law. For the rest of Elizabeth's reign the O'Cahans seem to have been on good terms with her representatives.

The McQuillans were still powerful at the close of the sixteenth century. They were an Anglo-Norman family, and had become more Irish than the Irish themselves. They held their lands by the point of the sword. The Lord Deputy wrote a letter to Henry VIII in 1542 in which St Leger claimed that McQuillan had informed him that not a chief of his clan had died in their beds, but that all had been slain by their enemies. The McQuillan had been in deadly conflict with the O'Cahans, and they met their match at the hands of the Scottish MacDonnells.

It has been pointed out that the MacDonnells of the Isles obtained land in County Antrim by the marriage of John Mor O'Donnell to Margaret Bisset, who, however, was of the Glens of Antrim. The MacDonnells now carried out extensive settlement in Antrim. It proved welcome, for times were difficult in Scotland. There were waves of settlement and they grew in power until by the middle of the sixteenth century they had become a formidable force. The English looked with apprehension at the MacDonnells settlement in North Antrim. Kenbaan Castle was built by Cola MacDonnell in 1547, and Dunangnore Castle about 1550 by his younger brother, Sorley Boy (Yellow Charlie). Sorley was one of the greatest MacDonnell leaders. He defended his heritage in the Glens of Antrim, and launched a force that would subject the Route

(North Antrim). Money was raised in Kintyre and the Isles. They sailed to Ballycastle Bay, which was protected by Sorley Boy's castle at Dunanynie. In the summer of 1559 Sorley attacked the McQuillans and a fierce battle was fought near Bonamargy at Ballycastle and up Glen of Glenskesk. The decisive battle was fought at Aura, a small stream which formed the boundary between the parishes of Armoy and Loughgnile. The McQuillans, however, were betrayed by a piper named O'Cahan, and they were eventually defeated. Sorley Boy now proceeded to seize the territory, and Dunluce Castle, pride of his possessions, fell under English rule.

In 1582 Marshal Bagenal looked at the McQuillan position. He said that the Route was fertile and pleasant, lying between the Glynns and the river Bann, and from Clandeboye to the sea. It was sometimes settled by the English, for there were the remains of a castle and monasteries. He said that the McQuillans now lay in waiting for the lands. The present holder, however, was a McQuillan, but the Scots had near expelled him into a small corner near the river Bann. He defended the position with the help of Turlough O'Neill. The Scots inhabited the rest of the lands using O'Neill's forces and not his own. Elizabeth's forces banished the Scots. Later McQuillan inherited the small Glenagherty Estate around Ballymena, but circumstances made him sell it off. The McQuillan of Wexford remained the representative of the McQuillans, one of whom recorded the history of the family from the year 1503.

A terrible event now took place: Ailhne, the O'Cahan chief, was drowned in the river Bann; he was the son of Cooey and grandson of Rory of the Route. He was succeeded by Rory, son of Manus and grandson of Donough. Parliament met at Dublin in 1585 and Rory attended. Some years later he provided refuge for 200 of Elizabeth I's troops. These troops had come from County Tyrone to fight against the O'Donnells. O'Donnell made a raid into Tyrone and all retreated before him to the Roe Valley. O'Neill and the English were assembled in the neighbourhood and O'Donnell marched to meet them, but they had to retreat into the castle on the river Roe, probably Limivady Castle. O'Donnell lay siege to it, but O'Cahan sent a messenger to O'Donnell reminding him that he was his foster father and that he had at all times been friendly with the O'Donnell family. He would protect those that had fled to the castle. He asked for the refugees and the spoils to be spared, and assured O'Donnell that this would not happen again. The request worked and O'Donnell was soon able to return to his own district.

In the final year of the sixteenth century, Hugh O'Neill revolted against the English. There were talks with the Crown and ceremonial fighting, but no settled agreement could be reached. In April 1598 the annalists record that the O'Cahan chief had died, and that his successor was his son, Donnell Ballagh. He entered upon his preferment with the knowledge that his clan had promised North Derry, and his ancestry could be traced back to Niall of the Nine Hostages in the fifth century. O'Neill was now convinced that it was time to rid Ireland, particularly Ulster, of English rule with the assistance of Spain. O'Neill broke off relations with the Crown and in the same year defeated the English at the Battle of Yellow Ford against Marshal Bagenal, who was killed in the field. O'Neill was hailed as saviour of his country. Queen Elizabeth was enraged at the losses on her side and looked about for a leader that would restore the status quo in Ireland. At this time O'Donnell Ballagh became chief, and he was to be the last chief of the name.

# Chapter 7

## *The O'Neill Wars*

O'Neill was now in the full tide of his fight against the English after the Battle of Yellow Ford. He had made ties with other chiefs in Ulster, thus reinforcing his position in the province. He had daughters married to Hugh Roe O'Donnell, Randal MacDonnell, Donnell Ballagh O'Cahan, Arthur Magennis, Hugh Maguire and other leaders in the north of Ireland. The English were demoralized. Queen Elizabeth was angry at the loss of her armies, and she sent her favourite, the Earl of Essex, to Ireland as Lord Lieutenant. Essex was armed with an effective force, and exclaimed that he would humble O'Neill, and win Ulster back, especially the Glens of Antrim, for the Queen. Garrisons were to be planted at Lough Neagh and Ballyshannon. But Essex lacked judgement. After playing with Hugh O'Neill he returned to England. He was replaced by Charles Blount, Lord Mountjoy, who arrived in Ireland in February 1600.

Essex had not liked the native people in Ulster, and Mountjoy used his knowledge to organize his campaign against the O'Neill. There were weaknesses to be observed on the Irish side, and Mountjoy was concerned how those weaknesses could be used against O'Neill. Essex suggested that ships should be sent to the coast to prevent powder and muskets reaching the insurgents from Scotland or Spain. Mountjoy said that the Irish could now storm a walled town or strong castle. He said that if his army were fed from England, and Ulster devastated, O'Neill would be starved into submission. Mountjoy's instructions had included the establishment of strongpoints at Lough Foyle and at Ballyshannon. The centre of Ulster was a vast wilderness of forest, bog and mountains and lacked an effective means of communication. It was inhabited by the most warlike of the Ulster clans. The policy was to feed Ulster by using sea power to supply Lough Foyle and to establish forts that could be held up the river by O'Neill in the east. The object of the Ballyshannon fort was to put an obstacle between O'Donnell's country and Connaught, which they often raided. The basic strategy was to place strongpoints to divide the northern clans from one another.

Fynes Moryson was Mountjoy's secretary, who mentions these garrisons as an important feature in the campaign. The insurgents could not leave them in the country to help each other in case the garrison would despoil it. He mentions the scorched earth policy suggested by Essex and how it was to be put into place by Mountjoy. It had been the policy to attack the rebels only in the summer. Mountjoy now attacked the clans in the winter also, being at least five days and a week in the saddle. The air was sharp and the Irish were naked. They were driven from their homes into the woods, bare of leaves. Their cattle were also driven to and fro, and they gave no milk in winter. They could not sow the ground, and at harvest time both Mountjoy's forces and the garrisons cut down their corn before it was ripe.

A third factor in the discontent was the use of important Irish figures in their own territories. Sir Neill Garve O'Donnell was promised the Lordship of Donegal, whilst Sir Arthur O'Neill was promised the Lordship of Tir-Owen (County Tyrone). Irishmen were recruited to fight against their own kind, and they were hated as much by the people they had betrayed as much by their old master. Fynes Moryson said that these Irish soldiers had borne the brunt of the fighting, and suffered much loss. Finally, some of the Gaels acted as spies and the information obtained was to determine the tactics to be employed. Mountjoy, however, reduced the discussion of complaints to a minimum and guarded against indiscretion in his entourage. He was using a lot of Irish troops so any careless folk might find themselves at the ear of Hugh O'Neill.

The new plan was put into operation in the spring of 1600. Ships were dispatched from England to assist the Lough Foyle force – a force that consisted of 4,000 foot and 200 horse. It was under the command of Sir Henry Docwra. It was also equipped with masons and carpenters to erect the necessary fortifications and homes for the garrison, with a great quantity of tools. Now Mountjoy marched in May in order to compromise with O'Neill and to give the Lough Foyle force time to dig in and prepare fortifications. Under cover of this feint, Docwra's forces established themselves at Lough Foyle on 14 May. There was a full tide, and the fleet weighed anchor and sailed a little way, but it ran aground. It was now the morning of the 16th, and the ships were able to set sail again about ten o'clock (one hundred men lying on the shore and giving a volley and retiring). The force landed at Culmore and the first horse and foot were landed. The main objective was to land the men; the landing of the horse was a secondary consideration. They built a fort at the end of the old broken castle to lodge, it was hoped, 200 men. Docwra described the situation. The piece of ground he obtained without resistance, and it was a fit place to make the main plantation/colonization. The region was dry and high and healthy to dwell upon. The castle was close to the waterside. He was determined to provide good ground for his ammunition and armaments. The walls of the cathedral-church stood nearby and another fort was erected to safeguard the situation.

The Annals also record Docwra's landing in Lough Foyle and the construction of three forts – at Dunnalong in O'Neill's part of his country in the neighbourhood of O'Cahan territory, at Culmore and at Derry. The construction of these forts was quite solid. They were mounds and great ramparts so that they faced the enemy in a position of strength. These constructions were of great value and were stronger than the materials that made up the stone cathedral. The rest of the ecclesiastical building in the area was used for living quarters. Docwra was a disgruntled knight but was of great wisdom and ingenuity. Six thousand men arrived upon the scene, and once they had arrived at Derry, they considered Culmore and Dunnalong of little consequence.

Now that Derry was chosen as the key base, building went on without great interruption. Shells for mortar were found in a little island at the mouth of the harbour, but the main demand was for timber. Ships were sent along the coast. If there were any houses left, they were to demolish them and bring back the timber and building materials. On O'Cahan's side there was a large coppice. There was plenty of birch, and Docwra sent men to cut it every day. He said that the working party had to have safe ground and there was not a stick of it brought home that was not fought over. Houses were erected with these materials, and the foundations of the plantation took shape. At first Docwra stood by his defences, probably fearing to be attacked by O'Neill's superior forces. The Annals of the Four Masters said that the English were in fear that some Irish had not shown themselves outside the ramparts, and a great number marched during the night. Upon taking stock of their position they were subject to sickness, which reduced their effectiveness. Many dropped dead in great numbers, but hundreds more were still of use for active service. However, Derry was defeated, and help for the Irish was required. Now the scorched earth policy was put into action. Docwra wrote by the end of the year, giving a description of Lough Foyle and the country adjoining. He had not too much of O'Cahan's territory and he said that the land was full of corn, with richer and more fertile soil than that of O'Doherty, which was of great extent.

Winter passed and O'Cahan approached Docwra saying that he was willing to surrender his lands, and to hold them from the Queen. These requests were probably made on numerous occasions, but were rejected by Docwra. Mountjoy said that this was standard procedure. Fynes Moryson said that protection and pardon was easily obtained for the rebels. They were willing to break their faith after submission in the hope of receiving money. They might plunge themselves into all sorts of mischief. They became poor and there was little chance of revolt.

On 7 March Sir John Bolles wrote to Cecil that the Irish should be brought in through the persuasion of priests, allowing them to monitor their strength and ability to resist. The second method of obtaining submission was to point out that the country had been so ravaged that resistance was no longer possible. As far as Bolles was concerned he had to keep the people from ploughing by dispersing the garrison, and force them to live within their means or to starve in the following years. From a military point of view this was sound common sense. This was a ruthless policy and would have long-term effects upon those they hoped to rule peaceably. In the same letter Bolles records the first of the major raids that occupied the second year. He said that they had obtained eighty lean cows and burned many houses, besides sheep and corn. Eighty to a hundred Gaels were put to the sword. This was in O'Cahan's country and the people fought with great fortitude. They had, in small number, marched five miles, but it was so cold at this time of year that they killed but one of the enemy and injured five.

There were now a series of raids on the lands of O'Cahan, a supporter of O'Neill, and an effort was made to subdue him. He was called obstinate, proud, a powerful rebel, and the greatest friend of O'Neill. Docwra was aware of the great advantage that they had. The Gaels had not the artillery like the English. They were well supplied with boats and ships and they could attack in the knowledge of an easy retreat. There were many landing places along the lough. Men of experience wondered why better use had not been made of the Derry force before this. Another raid was made on 25 March, and 300 cows had been captured, and an effort was made to bring them to Derry. Snow had fallen heavily; now this was melting in the spring, and the fords were overflowing with floodwater. Most of the cattle were lost in the crossing, and forty cattle had perished. On 2 April the garrison captured sixty cows from the O'Cahan side of the river.

The nature of the raids did not change, so that defensive policies were taken. On O'Cahan's side of the river the situation was keenly watched, and any movements were reported. Sir Arthur O'Neill recommended a raid be made from O'Doherty's country. Docwra agreed and posted out Sir John Chamberlain with 700 men. The men marched all night, crossed the river at Gleencastle; at daybreak, 10 June, they descended upon the many herds of cattle, which they drove to the Waterside. One hundred cows were loaded into the boats. Some were brought away dead, and the rest of the cattle were 'hackneyed and mangled'.

The way was now clear in June for a further effort in the campaign. O'Cahan's castle at Enagh Lough was seized. Docwra wrote a letter to the Privy Council about these events on 2 July 1601. He said that he had attacked O'Cahan's castle with cannon, but he was unable to capture Enagh in a single day. The night closed in, so he could withdraw his artillery. The men stole out about midnight, some by boat, others only swimming. The lough was large, and so left the castle in a good position. The castle was thought to be impregnable. He offered some terms of agreement. The capture of Enagh Castle gave the forces at Derry a foothold on O'Cahan's side of the river Foyle. It also provided a base for further operations.

During the summer the supply position of the Derry garrison determined Rory O'Cahan's position. He was the brother of the chief, Donnell Ballagh, and agreed to serve under Sir Arthur O'Neill. He arrived at Derry on 24 August, accompanied by four horsemen and thirty footmen together with a present of sixty fat cattle. Fresh meat was growing scarce, together with other provisions. The present was welcome and Rory made some money. Docwra supplied him with a small number of soldiers, and they returned the next day with forty more cattle. After another few days Rory brought in further cattle. He asked for 600 soldiers that would be of great service to Queen Elizabeth. Docwra was warned by Sir Arthur O'Neill to beware of him, but Docwra refused. Rory was allowed to depart leaving a few of his men as pledges for his return.

The following day Rory returned to the Waterside with 300 men. They kept the Foyle between them and sent word to Docwra that he was no longer willing to serve against his brother. He said that he would pay for the return of the hostages. He threatened that if the English took the lives of the hostages he would spare no Englishman who came within his jurisdiction. He refused any terms, and set up a gibbet upon which he hanged the hostages in sight of their leader. Perhaps Rory had been sent in to gain the confidence of the garrison. This would lead to him marching a large contingent into an ambush set by Hugh O'Neill. But the raiding party was not so successful as it first appeared. The reason for this was that, in a letter dated 2 September, the traitor O'Cahan would not compromise with the Crown. He said that if the governor, Docwra, would place at Coleraine a number of foot besides his own company, he would soon make him stop. If Docwra attacked him, then O'Cahan would launch a counter-attack. The English effort, now that it was August and September, was recoiling after setbacks. The Irish had the opportunity of launching a successful blow, but they failed to drive home their advantage. Mountjoy had marched north into Ulster, but he lacked support from Docwra, so his force had to retreat in the latter part of August without making a deep penetration into Tir-Owen.

Supplies had been running low at Derry. Docwra was in trouble, for he said that the winter had come fiercely upon them. The land was scattered with many sick men. All the biscuit had been eaten, and the provisions only consisted of meal, butter and a little wine. They could only hold out for six days. Derry was on the verge of being captured. On 16 September O'Donnell armed with 2,000 men, about midnight, marched to within a short distance of the fortifications. But his men fired too soon, and the garrison had time to prepare for an assault. The attacks, however, were not serious. The Gaels soon learnt that a Spanish fleet had entered Kinsale Harbour, and the Spanish troops were now preparing to fight for the Irish. If this force had arrived at Killybegs and had O'Donnell pressed his attack at Derry, the war might have turned out differently.

Derry survived with the arrival of fresh supplies, so that they could hold out in the face of the enemy. In the south-west of Ireland the Spanish landed, ready to fight for O'Neill. This was a considerable distance from Ulster. Hugh O'Neill and O'Donnell marched south to assist the Spanish. Kinsale was besieged by Mountjoy. O'Neill and O'Donnell were defeated by Mountjoy at the end of that year. Kinsale was evacuated by the Spanish and they returned to Spain with a safe conduct. Cecil wrote to Carew, saying that the agreement with the Spanish should be broken on the pretext that they had broken their side of the agreement. By this time the last of the Spaniards had retreated to Spain.

In County Derry O'Cahan prepared himself for another period of heavy attacks. He made an agreement with the MacDonnells of Antrim in regard to safety of their cattle. Each were afraid of raids – Docwra from Derry, MacDonnell from Carrickfergus. If the Governor of Carrickfergus raided the Route, the Scots were to drive their cattle into O'Cahan territory, near the river Bann. If Carew threatened O'Cahan, the cattle were to pass into the Route. Docwra heard this information and he was determined to plant a garrison at Coleraine. This would drive the Antrim MacDonnells from the O'Cahans, bringing about the wasting of crops and livestock in County Derry. It would also mean that there would be a military base from which to penetrate up the valley of the Bann to Dungiven, in Tir-Owen.

Docwra made a determined effort to carry out a plan towards the close of the year. In a letter of 6 December 1601, his plans are mentioned. This attack on the Gaels was similar to Clan Connor's conquest of the Cianachta. It was recommended that Clan Dermot should hold their position near Derry. At length the O'Cahans entered Cianachta via the

Bann Valley and the Creeve. This would all be a land operation. Docwra held a strong position at Enagh Lough, in order to use sea power in the war, to enter the river Bann and so plant the garrison at Coleraine. The necessary provisions were shipped and escorted down Lough Foyle, with a fair wind, before sailing himself. A double-pronged attack was then carried out. Captain Roger Orme was dispatched with 200 English, and the Gaels of Inishowen had to cross by boat from Greencastle into the protected side of O'Cahan's lands. Docwra took part in the attack by land himself. O'Doherty of course was on the English side. Docwra estimated Orme's force at 2,000 men. Without O'Doherty's help it would have been impossible to make an attack on any great scale.

Docwra and his men marched to the Common Wood, which stretched from Loughermore and held the entrance to the Roe Valley. Rory O'Cahan guarded the pass with 300 men. He advanced with some horsemen and fought some renegade Gaelic troops. Rory fell off his horse and started to run away. Edmund Groome leapt to his horse and pursued Rory and caught him by the collar. Edmund Groome refused a large ransom and delivered Rory to Docwra, and his soldiers were ordered to kill him – Sir Neill Grave O'Donnell called this a brutal murder.

Docwra disliked the passage through the woods; he preferred the lough side and this came into the district of the Roe Valley. He burned and spoiled everywhere he went. Orme had landed from Greencastle as planned. Even with the element of surprise there had been enough warning of their coming to enable the herds to be driven into the mountains. But only a few cattle were seized, the greater part of the spoil being sheep. Docwra and Orme met as planned and encamped in the centre of the district. The soldiers now proceeded to devastate the countryside, and Docwra described the event. O'Cahan's camp was also burned. The Roe Valley had so far escaped Docwra's forces. Ulster did not escape the scorched earth policy, and Mountjoy on one occasion brought with him scythes and sickles to lay waste the crops, but the larger part of the ground he gained had to be cut with swords. The harvest in the Roe Valley had been saved in spite of the operations, only to be burned before the worst of the weather came. The Gaels had now only their cattle left as a means of sustenance. The object of the exercise had failed. The sailors who were to meet Docwra at Coleraine missed the town. Docwra waited one night at Coleraine and when the ships did not appear he marched southwards up the Bann Valley, with a view to devastating the land as far as Dungannon. There had been snow and frost, so he decided to retreat to Derry. There was now a sudden thaw. Docwra returned at the end of November, with fresh determination to plant a garrison at Coleraine where opportunity knocked. Chichester was also aware of the strategic importance of Coleraine. In January 1602 he wrote to Cecil saying that Sir Henry Docwra intended to settle at Coleraine on O'Cahan's side, and that Chichester should do the same on this side of the Route, but he said that they had not the necessary tools. The place should be victualled from the sea. From Coleraine it was an easy march to Dungannon, by passing up the river Bann.

A hard winter came, and the Spanish forces left Munster. The prospect for the success of Irish troops was not great, and O'Cahan asked for a surrender. On 11 March 1602 Sir Henry Docwra wrote to the Privy Council, explaining the conditions that he had discovered. Absolute submission to Elizabeth was required as well as the bringing in of cattle to a place appointed by Sir Henry. The Enagh garrison was to prove a welcome addition to his policies. A list of all able-bodied men was requested and the surrender of six pledges, O'Cahan's son being one. O'Cahan, probably fearing a trap, did not turn up at Enagh.

The talks might not be successful, and Docwra attempted to garrison Coleraine. Stores for the operation were put aboard ship. There was a good wind and the ships would meet the land forces at the mouth of the river Bann. Spies had also been sent within O'Cahan's and Tyrone's territory, to find out what forces O'Cahan had available, or whether he would receive help from the O'Neill. Some of these forces returned before the land forces left Enagh. Other soldiers, however, met these forces as they advanced four miles from Enagh to within two miles of O'Cahan's camp. The English wanted an immediate answer to their proposals. O'Cahan wanted a truce for three months and he tried to persuade Docwra to secure this. Meanwhile O'Cahan remained encamped at the mouth of a pass through the forests with 600 foot and sixty horse.

The captains of the English forces were asked for their views as to whether they should force the pass and proceed with the long-delayed plan of garrisoning Coleraine. The captains thought that they should be able to have forced the pass through the common ground, but there were other factors that had to be taken into account – the loss of ammunition, the casualties, the necessity of leaving a garrison of one hundred men at the river Bann.

There was also the likelihood of reinforcements reaching O'Cahan. Their return might be in jeopardy, and it was resolved not to make an attempt, but to wait for a more convenient time. The land forces had failed to make the rendezvous, and Docwra must have been aware that he was himself open to serious criticism for not taking advantage of the moment. He had sent a memorandum to the captains, giving his reasons for not implementing the plan.

O'Cahan tried to bribe Docwra, but he did not bite. Docwra said that he had sent out Captain Badby and Captain Windsor in succession on one of each of the following nights. They had been sent into his territory to take prey. Badby advanced up to sixteen miles, took 160 cows and killed thirty people. Windsor advanced up to twenty miles, and killed one hundred of them, including those chief men of account, 'many kerne, the churls, women and children'. He drove off some twenty cows. He said that the country was in a state of famine as a result of the English raids, so the poor were in a terrible state and the rich were reduced. They asked for Spanish help in the way of more reinforcements. Otherwise they would have to submit, or at worst be prepared against a couple of months' campaign against them. The wood kerne and other outlaws were numerous and they fell back upon the disorganization of the countryside.

The campaign was ruthless, as seen in Docwra's writings. The kerne were not well armed and the churls were the workers on the farmlands. But none of these two groups were spared the English yoke. There were those that were still not satisfied with the resultant destitution to which a settled and industrious people had been reduced. A Captain Thomas Phillips had just left Carrick on the shores of Belfast Lough to meet Chichester and wrote to Cecil on the same date, 11 March 1602. He supported the idea of a Coleraine garrison which would thwart O'Neill and that he had been chosen by the Lord Deputy for the initial colonization/plantation. He opposed the idea of settlement with O'Cahan. It was reputed that O'Cahan wanted to approach Elizabeth, and so would all his supporters if given permission. They did this in order to save their goods and to keep them might lead to another war, for the Gaels were all but starving. Phillips had his eyes upon the lands of the north, and any agreement reached with O'Cahan would leave him in quiet possession of his lands. This would not have been a welcomed agreement.

O'Cahan's resistance changed in the month ahead, and Docwra said that on 12 April he made an agreement with Cane Ballogh MacRichard, a chief of the O'Cahan country, delivering to him the castle of Dungiven, situated on the Glinnes and about eighteen miles from Derry. At the end of the war he gave his word that the castle would be restored again. The English realized the importance of Dungiven, commanded by the Glen Shane Pass and also by the woods of Glenconkeyne. He wrote later that he had captured Dungiven Castle from O'Cahan.

After two years the countryside had been reduced to an unacceptable state. Fynes Moryson said that there was the spectacle of the reduced farms, especially those that had been devastated. The people had to eat nettles and docks, and their lips were green. By now Docwra had taken Omagh, and had been fortifying it. Mountjoy went north, passing through Dungannon, and Chichester and Docwra met him for a conference at the end of June. They realized the importance of the situation, and Docwra said that he would try his best to cope. Mountjoy wrote to the Privy Council on 29 June that O'Neill was holding out in what seemed to be an impregnable position in County Tyrone, so that it was impossible to launch an attack upon him. But the English were sure that O'Neill would eventually have to flee the country. O'Neill was on O'Cahan's lands, where he now had organized his attack upon English rule, not only in Ulster but in the rest of Ireland.

O'Cahan had written to Chichester, begging terms. He had the reply that his surrender was accepted on condition that he would not attack Queen Elizabeth. O'Neill, O'Donnell and the Scots of Antrim had no other choice but to be on Docwra's side. He ended by saying that when he gave the word it would be between himself and God if he broke it. In a private message by word of mouth he offered Elizabeth loyal service, particularly military help when requested. He wanted a quick reply, but the offer of surrender was refused. On 14 July, Docwra wrote that he had social relations with O'Neill, and that the negotiations with him were successful, and the articles of agreement were signed. This was a very important agreement. O'Cahan and his followers were to be pardoned for all former offences. Coyne Ballagh O'Cahan was to remain in possession of quite a lot of territory around Dungiven, which he and his kin had won by the sword. The land was held from Elizabeth, and was not dependent upon O'Cahan. There was a garrison here and Coyne Ballagh had to find opportunities elsewhere, for Coyne Ballagh was an honest man. (He was the grandson of O'Donnell the Cleric and a second cousin of Rory, father of the present chief, Donnell Ballagh.) The land between the river Faughan and Lough Foyle was to be surrendered to Her Majesty, as well as church lands. The land surrounding Enagh, and a ballybooe at Coleraine for the garrison there, were also reserved. Elizabeth controlled the fishing along the Bann and the Faughan. The spy and guide, Dennis O'Mullan, was to have a piece of land, as agreed between O'Cahan and Docwra. O'Cahan was now to have a proper title from the Queen for the remainder of his lands. Pledges were made for the observance of these conditions by O'Cahan, not only for himself but for other notables around the island.

O'Cahan kept his part of the agreement. He sent two persons to Dublin to ask for the performance of the other sides of the agreement – for example, the re-grant of his lands under letters patent from Elizabeth. On 11 October, the Lord Deputy and his council wrote to the English Privy Council, saying that they had the authority from Queen Elizabeth to make such a re-grant, but in the meanwhile he was left as custodian of his part of the country under the Great Seal of Ireland until the Queen granted him more land. O'Cahan's example created a good deal of respect for he had fulfilled his part of the agreement.

In 1602, on 20 October, Donnell O'Cahan, chief of his clan, was granted primacy in his country, except for the territories that he had surrendered in the agreement. No letters patent for the lands were given and this was one of the conditions upon which O'Cahan surrendered. His pardon was granted on 20 October, and involved about twenty people. O'Cahan was left to himself, with his wife (Rosa O'Neale), Rowrie O'Cahan (his son), Grany O'Cahan (his daughter) and all of his other children. Also involved was Donough McRedie, priest of Donald O'Cahan, the Dean of Derry. Being lodged in Dublin Castle he was later apprehended. O'Cahan wanted to be free of any allegiance he had paid to O'Neill, and he preferred to hold his land directly from the Queen. He also obtained a pledge from Docwra and Mountjoy concerning the pledge, and he also asked Docwra to write to O'Neill. O'Neill replied; but if he were accepted, O'Cahan would be taken out of a dependent position.

At the close of the previous August, the Lord Deputy had advanced northwards again to devastate the land and to destroy O'Neill's harvest. He destroyed the stone chair used for the inauguration of the O'Neill. The famine was fierce; corpses lay everywhere. Mountjoy wrote to O'Hagan that between Tullyhog and Toome there lay unburied 1,000 dead. The northward march had promised a success for the English, but its long-term effects on Gaelic-English relations leaves much to be desired.

Rory O'Donnell, now head of his clan, surrendered in November. The Lord Deputy recommended to Elizabeth and her council that Donegal should be divided between Rory and Neill Garve O'Donnell. O'Donnell had been promised the whole of Donegal, and his help was not forgotten to the Lough Foyle force. The pledge was now treated as a sixteenth century 'scrap of paper' to be torn up by the clan, and this was an indication of what was to come. O'Neill, in March, surrendered to Mountjoy. The deputy granted him freedom in the Queen's name, restoration of his Earldom of Tyrone, and letters patent for all his lands except districts possessed by two kinsmen. There was also 300 acres attached to the forts of Mountnorris and Charlemont. But Elizabeth died, and the new king, James I, of the House of Stewart, Scotland, granted O'Neill the lands that belonged to his grandfather, Con; by this Tyrone thought that his lands would violate O'Cahan's country. Rory O'Donnell was created Earl of Tyrconnell, but Neill Garve was awarded no fresh lands. Docwra now had an extensive interview with the Lord Deputy, and said that O'Cahan should be subject to Tyrone (O'Neill).

Docwra ceased to press the matter and eventually made tracks for

Derry with the Earl of Tyrone's eldest son. Docwra undertook to inform O'Cahan of how the matter stood. O'Cahan did not like the news, pointing out his loyalty to England since he had surrendered, and said that the breaking of the pledges upon which he relied had left him in a sorry state. He saw no remedy. O'Cahan pointed out that he had not received a clear title to his lands from the Crown, and was left to deal with O'Neill, who was determined to treat O'Cahan as a tenant at will at whatever rent O'Neill chose to levy. In a letter O'Neill stated that he wanted a rent of 160 cows. He also wanted the lands lying between the river Bann and the north-east of the Roe Valley. At length an agreement was reached whereby O'Neill took one third of O'Cahan's country, leaving O'Cahan with two-thirds. Docwra said that O'Cahan had received a written grant of his lands from Tyrone (O'Neill).

O'Cahan found him in ever increasing difficulty. The Bishop of Derry, George Montgomery, was trying to obtain lands within his district, which he said belonged to the bishopric. O'Cahan was now urged to take back his former wife on the grounds that he had never been legally separated from her. If O'Cahan did this, he feared that Tyrone might invade his country to obtain the dowry that went with O'Cahan's present wife, O'Neill's daughter. By October 1606 matters came to a head, for O'Neill now stole many cattle that belonged to O'Cahan. O'Cahan now tried to obtain his lands by legal means. In May 1607, he petitioned the Lord Deputy, setting out his grievances. On 1 June, Sir Oliver St John wrote to Salisbury outlining the situation, recalling the pledges that O'Cahan had received, and the importance of the support that O'Cahan had given O'Neill. He had stated that St John had said to O'Neill that O'Cahan should take up residence at the head of the clan. There would be enough native or English freeholders to set up a major plantation.

O'Cahan's position was considered by the Irish Privy Council. Although the idea was welcome, nothing transpired. O'Cahan thought that he might obtain at least a part of what he had been promised. He had received a knighthood in June 1607. Now three months later a dramatic event took place. On 14 September, O'Neill and the other clans set sail from Lough Swilley to seek asylum on the Continent. The lands of Rory O'Donnell were declared forfeit. Settlers from England and Scotland would inherit the clansmen's lands and set up their little houses. They would remain a check to any Irish uprising. There were wider plans afoot, for O'Cahan stood in the way of the English colonizers of the province. The Bishop of Derry told Salisbury that O'Cahan held his possessions by a long tradition. O'Cahan's intentions were now suspicious.

Sir George Paulet now became Governor of Derry, and he wrote to the Lord Deputy voicing his suspicions. He wrote that O'Cahan had many close followers. It was later stated that Sir Donnell O'Cahan was in his territory close to Londonderry. He exclaimed that no Englishman or Scotsman should attack him. Perhaps he feared arrest, but he was in the position whereby an official summons probably meant arrest. To refuse arrest was tantamount to disloyalty. Sir Thomas Phillips apprehended him in February 1608. He was charged with treason. On 17 February, Chichester wrote to Salisbury that Sir Donnell O'Cahan was charged with an offence and that he could not clear himself. He was housed in Dublin Castle, but he said that his son was brought up to be a learned gentleman. The Lord's council wrote to Chichester approaching his actions and giving him an inkling of what was going on. It was clear that O'Cahan's land was of the most importance and they were determined to colonize it. Chichester wrote again to the Privy Council asking whether to charge O'Cahan and bring him to court, or to confirm that he should hold his lands.

The countryside had not recovered from the devastation, especially in the early years. Chichester said that O'Cahan's country was now poor, and that he had little cattle or money to support himself. He could not employ his servants whilst he was in prison for he had been detained by the sheriff. Chichester had to supply O'Cahan's wants whilst he was in jail. He was successful in doing so and he reported that in the same year he had let Sir Donnell's lands for £330 per annum. He was anxious that he should pay this money for the support that he had asked, or to hand the land over to the state. Chichester mentioned that the chief source of income lay in their money receipts. The provisions of meat, butter, etc. were offered to the lucky. Rents would not be paid when they were in prison or absent.

There was also some excuse to keep Sir Donnell in prison. In 1608 his brother, Shane Garragh, made accusations against him, and took part in a rising. Other accusations were made against him, by Manus and others. There were six points of treason, the chief being that he wanted to go with O'Neill and that he had been engaged with Shane Garragh. However, it was doubtful if any jury would convict him on the evidence at hand, and no case was ever brought.

In June 1608, the Lord Deputy recommended Shane's release, since he had offered the surrender of Limavady Castle, and to capture his brother, Shane Garragh, dead or alive, and to look after his lands and subjects.

Now elaborate schemes were afoot. Chichester's policy on the plantation/colonization of Ulster had been prepared, dated 10 March 1608. The O'Cahan, O'Neills, Dennis Mullan, and others who had served in the English forces, should be awarded small portions. The scheme gradually got under way. All that now remained was for his paper planning to be put into action. But Sir Donnell had been lodged in Dublin Castle until July 1609. He was now imprisoned in the Tower of London. With his release a cruel aspect of English policy had been closed.

# Chapter 8

## *Colonization*

The way was now clear for the plantation of Ulster, and Sir Henry Docwra was succeeded as Governor of Londonderry by Sir George Paulet, a quick-tempered and rough representative. He guarded the young Sir Cahir O'Doherty of Inishowen, who rose in rebellion in April 1608. Cahir's men had rendered important the conquest of Derry, which was burnt and seized together with Culmore Fort. Sir Cahir's country was conquered and within three months he himself had been killed, and his head stuck on the city gates of Dublin. There were two other knights that had been promised for surrender – Sir Neill Garve O'Donnell and Sir Donnell O'Cahan who were destined for imprisonment in the Tower of London.

Chichester was, in October 1608, head of the plantation scheme in Ulster. The chief septs that occupied County Coleraine were the O'Cahans and under them the O'Mullans, the Magilligans and the McCloskeys. The main points that had to be taken were the castles of Limavady, Enagh, Coleraine and Dungiven. He remembered that most of the castles had been in ruins and out of repair. He said that if Sir Donnell O'Cahan be released two parts of the country would not satisfy him – nor indeed all. It is not clear what became of him, but due consideration must be made for his brother Manus, Manus McCowy Ballagh and a few others that had survived the troubles before Nealle King petitioned the Crown. He had at a later date carried arms and ammunition to Manus O'Cahan and the Scots of Enagh. They had killed many of the enemy, and claimed that during O'Doherty's rebellion he – King – had encouraged two gentlemen of County Coleraine to serve in Captain Manus O'Cahan's company, where they performed well.

An insight into conditions is given in a letter by Sir Robert Jacob to Salisbury which stated that they had crossed the river Bann and entered County Coleraine, called O'Cahan's country, where sessions were held at Limavady, O'Cahan's headquarters, but this was a ruined castle. The land was poor in the vicinity. The people, it was recorded, were likely to rise and attack at any time, but they were still at peace. There were various people who lived between Dungiven Castle and Glenconcane. Captain Darlington was aware of the frontier men at Dungannon, and he was intent upon getting rid of hangers-on. The country lay all around Lough Foyle, where there are woods, and where the passes are kept clean.

In July 1609, Sir Donnell O'Cahan was sent to England and the Tower of London. In the same summer a commission was established to delve into the fortified lands in the six Ulster counties of Armagh, Tyrone, Coleraine, Donegal, Fermanagh and Cavan. Antrim, Down and Monaghan were left out. The commission started from London near the end of July and they made enquiries at Armagh and Dungannon before setting out for O'Cahan's country. The commissioners emerged from the forests into the Roe Valley on 27 August. They had camped for three nights en route. They reached Limivady and encamped about a mile distant. The inquisition to distinguish between Church and Crown lands was convened at Limavady on Wednesday 30 August. The jury consisted of fifteen men from the county who were clerks and scholars. Thirteen of them spoke Latin well. They gave their verdict in good time and provided the commissioners with more light about the origins of the Church lands. They discovered that the lands of some families were theirs by right, and that the Bishop was only one of them. The Bishop of Derry was greedy for land. He tried to coerce the jury to deliver a favourable verdict.

The jury was divided into families. There arrived at Limavady four agents from the City of London, and they would review O'Cahan's country together with Sir Thomas Phillips. Phillips had been in the army at the end of Elizabeth's reign. He was eventually raised to be military superintendent of the County of Coleraine and the lands of Glenkonkeyne. He was an all-rounder – he had a great capacity for business and had encouraged a small colony at Coleraine. Phillips now showed the colonizers the prime parts of the country, avoiding the Sperrin Mountains and lesser attractive districts. These people reported to London at the close of the year. They were granted the whole of County Coleraine and the Barony of Loughinsolin, which contained the great woods of Glenconkeyne and Killetragh as well as the lands west of the Foyle, near Derry (Londonderry). The conditions stated that there should be a settlement in the region of sixty houses at Derry and forty at Coleraine. In such a manner had the modern County Londonderry taken shape, with the forty houses at Coleraine and Derry providing a home for the planter on the surrounding lands. At the time of the conquest, O'Cahan's country at Coleraine and Derry were deemed to be of great strategic significance. Loughinsolin was taken out of Tyrone and the liberties of Derry and

Coleraine from Donegal and County Antrim. Church lands were excepted from the Londoner's grants, lands intended for native freeholders. There was an important grant to Phillips in the area of the Roe Valley which was called the 'Garden of the North'.

Sir Donnell O'Cahan wrote to Salisbury in March 1610. He explained that he was coming to Dublin so that he could complain of injuries he sustained and that he had been taken prisoner. He said that he did not know why. He was threatened with treason. His wife and children had been thrust out of the house, and took to begging. He had appealed to the King and Council and said that he was innocent. At the same time Sir Donnell said that he had claimed that he had entrusted one Rice Gilmore with his affairs and had given him money to do this. He said that Gilmore had done nothing for him, but he was given an option on O'Cahan's lands and kept his money. Sir Donnell was made sheriff of the county and held a number of cattle at his castles. He drove out his wife and children, one of whom was almost drowned in a dike. Gilmore carried out his threats in spite of the Lord Deputy's warrant, which Sir Donnell possessed for his lands, houses and moveables.

On 1 June 1610, he wrote from the Tower of London to obtain his release. The letter was very pessimistic, but he protested his innocence. He went on to say that his death might be welcomed rather than his release. He signed the letter his 'loving brother – The Tower, 1 June, 1610'. Manus was not in a hurry to help. He handed over the letter of his brother to Chichester. He was ever anxious to learn of any communications that Irish prisoners in the Tower had without its walls.

In September 1612, the Lord Deputy wrote to the Privy Seal stating that about two years previously he had come across letters written from Sir Donnell O'Cahan to Manus, his brother. In the letters he exclaimed he had admiration for the English nation, and he laboured to make his people more pliable to the Irish folk and to incite O'Cahan to oppose any efforts at plantation. Desire for land might influence his brother's actions and Sir Donnell was not too far away.

On 16 August 1611, one John Rowley and Tristram Beresford, who were agents for the City of London, allotted thirteen freeholds to the Gaels – five major freeholders and eight smaller ones. The key freeholders were: Captain Manus O'Cahan, 2,000 acres; Lady O'Cahan with her son, 1,000 acres; Cowy Ballagh McRichard O'Cahan, 1,000 acres; Tomlyn and Owen Keogh O'Mullan, 500 acres.

Manus was granted important lands in the parish of Faughanvale and Glendermot near Derry. The lands of the two O'Mullans were in the parish of Cumber and Banagher and lay near Sawel Mountain. Cowy Ballagh McRichard's lands were in the parish of Bovevagh near

Dungiven. The land was settled with the Lord Deputy's permission in April 1602. Manus McCowey Ballagh received his lands in Coleraine barony; his ancestry dated back to the chieftain of the O'Cahans in the fifteenth century. At length the title passed on to Sean. Lady O'Cahan's lands lay in the western foothills of a ridge running from Keady towards Donald's Hill.

There were eight other freeholders, ranging from Gorry McShane O'Cahan in the parish of Banagher, to Gillduffe Oge O'Mullan in the parish of Dungiven. One James McGorry obtained the island of Loughan and other lands in the parish of Ballyrashane.

Carew now surveyed the districts to be settled by the landowners, who made a slow progress. Sir Thomas Phillips, who had surrendered his position at Coleraine, was now proceeding with great energy in the Limavady area. He had erected a watermill, which had a sluice a mile long, the Roe mill that remained was the manor mill. Here tenants could grind their own corn during succeeding generations. He also built a mill for the use of travellers, which was two-storeyed, forty-four feet long and seventeen feet broad. A lot of timber had been felled in the forest of Glenconkeyne. Sir Donnell O'Cahan's former home, Limavady Castle, together with other buildings, also came under review. Stone was quarried from the hard rocks of the ditch near the castle, and was earmarked as a defence work.

Captain Edward Doddington was equally enterprising. A few of the walls at Dungiven Castle were still standing, and Doddington built it into a castle four storeys high, twenty-two feet wide, well finished and slated. He had repaired the stone and lime bawn (small manor house) which was for defensive purposes. This cost him £300 of his own money as well as £200 he had received from the Crown for the repair of the castle and bawn.

A wall of earth and sods, sixteen feet high and twelve to fourteen feet thick had been built up around Coleraine Castle with bulwarks of the same height, but it was not a substantial form of fotification. Pynnar's survey of 1618–19 showed that the walls and ramparts were starting to decay, and the bulwarks were so small that artillery could not be set upon them. Derry had been fortified at a later date than Coleraine and in a more interesting style. There was a wall of lime and stone twenty-one feet high and six feet thick, with four gates. There were also nine large bulwarks, suitable for artillery. The rampart within the city was twelve feet thick and made of earth.

Sir Thomas Phillips received a grant from the Crown in 1612 at a minimal rent of sixpence, and this was one of the wealthiest agricultural districts in the nine counties of Ulster. The lands around Limavady centred around O'Cahan's castle on the Roe, a place now known as Kane's Rock. On the Derry side of the Roe, his estates stretched from Drumraigh and Ballymore through Clogher, Tallaght and Drumballydonaghy to the field of Lomond and Myroe. To the east of the Roe, his lands stretched down through Terrydremond to the lands where the town now stands. The lands had begun at Ballyquin. East of the town his estates stretched out through Killane to Derrymore and Derrybeg. He was granted O'Cahan's castle, and the state papers record how well he managed the situation, renovating the castle for defence purposes. The town had a drawbridge, moat and circular tower. It was provided with two field guns. Beyond the castle Sir Thomas built his own house, made out of stone with a slated roof. It was blessed with an orchard, gardens, doves and pigeons. It should be remembered that these achievements were brought about by his own efforts and not by the O'Cahan. Limavady is indebted to Sir Thomas as a builder of this townland. About a mile from the town lay the old town of Limavady, where he had built a village of eighteen small houses. The village boasted a stone cross at its centre. This town bears the name Newtown-Limavady. Around the Roe mill there was some activity, with a considerable number of houses. The church at Drumachose ruin still stands beside the road to Coleraine and Garvagh. People worshipped in the houses of the new town and some of the earliest settlers were made up of twenty-five families which Sir Thomas had brought from England.

The purpose of the Scots colonization was to plant the maximum number of people on the land with English and Lowland Scots tenants who would provide a permanent check on rebellion. The companies' lands were to be occupied only with these chosen tenants. Phillips was permitted to take native Gaels and their tenants to Church lands, for example the Magilligan district. All Irish were to be removed from the lands of the London companies by 1 May 1612, but the date had to be reviewed, for there were not sufficient colonizers available to farm the lands. However, the original plan was carried out to some considerable extent.

In origin the plantation/colonization of Ulster was an attempt to plant Ulster with tenants who would be more co-operative with the native Gaels. It was a great effort to bring this about, to change the way people lived. Land ownership was to be changed and farmers were to bow to the Crown. English law was to replace Gaelic law and the Gaelic language. Houses were to be erected in the English fashion and not in an altered Gaelic style. Roman Catholicism was to be proscribed and replaced by the Church of England and the Church of Scotland. The practice of 'croughting' (using cattle for different purposes) was to end. Also to be condemned was the practice of 'commyns' where chiefs and other notables sent these cattle to graze on the lands of poor folk who had not, however, sufficient stock. These important men had riches in the way of large herds of cattle. In this way the whole Gaelic life was disrupted.

In July 1613 the Council of London wrote to Chichester saying that the wife of Sir Donnell O'Cahan had stayed for a long period in London and that they were returning to Ireland and asked for the cost of the journey, for they had exhausted their means in terms of 'commins'. Some of their tenants had refused to pay them. Chichester was of the opinion that they should have a place in Ireland and that any money due should fall to them. They should not return to London if the Council saw their complaints upsetting the distinguished knights in the Tower of London.

Chichester wrote to Sir Donnell O'Cahan enclosing a list of tenants to whom he had given cattle, the majority of which were O'Mullan's. Both he and his wife were in bad straits. Forty cows were to pay a debt owed to Sir Donnell, and the majority of his cattle he signed over to his sons, Rory and Donnell. A list of tenants was made from which cows were to be recovered to pay debts ranging from Fardoragh McBrian O'Moilan, five cows; to Torrilagh Balue O'Cuicke and brethren, two cows. Fardoragh is mentioned as head of the O'Mullans. The Quiggs are also mentioned as gallowglasses. Four years later a letter mentions Sir Donnell O'Cahan as appointing Carmocke O'Mullan to look after the property of Lady O'Cahan and her son Donnell. The letter stated that Carmocke was not to be given possession of land until he had spoken with Lady O'Cahan. He was to find out whether she was satisfied with the existing state of affairs; Carmocke should be put in charge of the land. If she did not like the choice for the land, then she was bound to name another man of sufficient standing.

About 1617, the O'Mullans were still in possession of the many lands west of Keady and Donald's Hill, even though most had the status of tenants. A list was drawn up for the half year from November 1616 to May 1617 to manage Lady O'Cahan's estates, among them the townland of Balle McGilgin and Balle Castlane. These were the tenants on the Haberdashers' estate.

There was a considerable amount of land belonging to Tomlin, Brian, Edmund Grome Donnell, and James and Brian McShane Boy – all these were O'Mullans. The castle of the Haberdashers lay in the northern portion, where it was built at Ballycastle and occupied by Sir Robert McClelland. The Fishmongers occupied land across the river Roe, having a castle at Ballykelly. The Skinners occupied land, having its castle at Dungiven. There was a castle belonging to the Darlingtons, and there was one at Crossalt. Magilligan was Church land, and the Gage family settled at Ballavena, rented from the Bishop of Derry in 1622. The manor house was quite old, and is one of the biggest houses in the country, dating back to about 1700. Marianne Gage, heir to the estate, married Sir Frederick William Heygate in 1581. The Clothworkers occupied the land at Magilligan, stretching into Killowen, with a castle two miles away. Next in size came the estate of the Merchant Tailors, whose headquarters was at Macosquin. Farther south were the Ironmongers whose estates lay in the Aghadowey and Garvagh districts. Their agents were the Cannings, and in 1818 George Canning was created Lord Garvagh. Beyond those estates lay the Mercers' lands around Kilrea.

The Vintners', Drapers' and Salters' lands lay in South Derry. The names Draperstown and Saltersland describe the connection with the estate companies. The land of the Grocers and Goldsmiths lay near Londonderry. The Goldsmiths' land lay in the Glenermott area while the Grocers built Muff, now the village of Eglintron. The estates in South Derry lay in O'Neill's territory. All these estates grew up more or less on what was O'Cahan's country, a few years before. The last O'Cahan chief, Sir Donnell, died in the Tower of London in 1628, after twenty years' imprisonment. He had refused to keep his pledges, and if he had done so, it is impossible to speculate upon his fate. Chichester had said to him that Sir Donnell was a man who kept his word, inactive as he may have been. The Reverend George Hill sized him up as a man of a fickle and selfish disposition, who did not like disappointments, and that he could not stand anyone else trying to settle on his land.

Sir Donnell's bard composed an elegy about him, bemoaning his imprisonment and praising his expertise in arms. The elegy verged on the side of flattery.

# Chapter 9

## *The Most Warlike Clans*

O'Cahan was reckoned to be the leader of the most warlike clans in Ulster at the time of the plantation/colonization. The Bishop of Derry wrote to Salisbury in 1607 saying that O'Neill, Earl of Tyrone, had at his disposal 200 foot and 300 horse, made up of the ablest men in Ulster. Hill quotes a passage made by the London companies who were pressed to make a plantation there. Hill suggests that there was a fear that Sir Donnell O'Cahan might return, and that his followers would not be pleasant neighbours.

The northern clans were poorly organized as far as arms and artillery were concerned. The scorched earth policy was followed by a policy of divide and rule by the English Government. The Irish of Inishowen and others aided the Crown. Spies and guides helped to make up the English troops. Docwra's letter dated 1 March 1602 to the English Privy Council is very interesting for it shows how dependent he was on his intelligence system. Docwra had spies in County Tyrone to discover whether O'Neill was sending O'Cahan reinforcements. He had spies in O'Cahan's camp so that he could estimate the total strength of his forces. Docwra now decided upon what policies he should pursue.

At the end of the wars O'Neill was restored to his title of Earl of Tyrone, but his spies now found themselves in difficulties. They were not allowed to return to their lands, which they had previously occupied. Docwra pleaded for the promises of O'Neill to be carried out and he brought up the case of the spies to Mountjoy. He failed to obtain any satisfaction in O'Cahan's case, but lands were found for the guides. He told Mountjoy of the services many of them had rendered, but the Gaels were destitute, and Docwra wanted something more enduring. Mountjoy said he would speak to O'Neill about these matters. Mountjoy said that one guide had been hanged by O'Neill. Docwra produced forthwith the evidence of prisoners in his keeping to assert his position. The whole matter stank and he asserted that it would be so offensive to the Lord Deputy.

The most experienced spy was one Dennis Mullan, and he was in a better position than his fellow spies. He appears on the list of army personnel on 23 July 1604 as a captain of thirty Irish foot, but the troop was reduced in January. Some think that Mullan had a house in Londonderry and permanent provision was made for him in 1604. As a return for his services Sir Henry Docwra persuaded the Earl of Tyrone and O'Cahan to pass into his freehold property without payment of any other rents and customs other than 12d per annum to the chief lord.

Mullan was a busy man. If the pledges made to Sir Donnell O'Cahan had been kept, events might have turned out differently. From the aristocracy to the Gaelic peasant there was disappointment everywhere. The scorched earth policy was pursued everywhere from 1600 to 1602 and had given rise to great resentment, which was felt like an underground bog fire. Trouble started in 1607 with the Flight of the Earls to Europe that September, which gave rise to uncertainties in Gaelic quarters and happiness in English ones. Chichester wrote to the Privy Council that O'Neill might try to return to Tyrone with foreign help. Many of the Gaels withdrew into the forests and fastnesses where they armed themselves as best they could. Inklings of insurrection were carefully observed by Dublin Castle. Shane Carragh O'Cahan, Sir Donnell's brother, burned some houses, this being a course of action followed by those who wanted to engage in open conflict. Shane Carragh endorsed the activities when Shane came for all intents and purposes an outlaw at the head of a number of wood kerne. Shane gave evidence against his brother in March 1608. Chichester wrote to the Privy Council on 2 April, submitting the confessions of Shane and a subsequent witness against Sir Donnell. This transpired before Shane went into upon rebellion.

Now O'Doherty was incited into rebellion and he seized Culmore and Derry. On 10 May Sir Thomas Phillips wrote to Salisbury that on Saturday, 7 May Shane Carragh, O'Cahan's brother, came to him. He had twenty men in his pay. He feared him and gave him some presents. O'Doherty set upon Dennis Mac O'Mullan, whom they had employed for a long time and put him to death along with others. They were now in open rebellion. There was now only one left in the territory, one Manus O'Cahan (O'Cahan's brother), and they expected news from him shortly. The two O'Mullans, Captain Dennis and Shane, were regarded by the English as faithful to the state, and by the Irish they were regarded as renegades. However, there was not a general insurrection and those involved were quickly captured or killed by other Irishmen. O'Doherty met his death at the hands of Irish soldiers who wanted his lands. Shane

Carragh, the main rebel in North Down, was captured by Hugh McShane and his brother, dwelling in the forests and glens of Tyrone. They had no love of English authority, but a proclamation was made by Chichester, promising free pardon for all those that surrendered. The McShanes pounced upon Shane Carragh and his companions. He killed ten or twelve of his men, taking him prisoner and dispatched him to the fort of Mountjoy. Rebels now came in freely by the middle of the summer – some were executed and some were subjected to trial by jury. Shane Carragh was tried at Dungannon by an Irish jury. He was found guilty and hanged.

Not all of the rebels were executed. A large number of men were shipped from Lough Foyle to Sweden. Then followed insurrection. In one stage during the plan for plantation the children of Dennis and Shane were to be looked after. But this may not have been carried out. The only divided freehold was the biggest one and some 500 in the lands were to be known as Ballymullans. The land was granted to Tomlyn and Owen Keogh O'Mullan. But it transpired that the lands were not suitable for plantation. After the rising of O'Doherty and Shane Carragh O'Cahan, discontent smouldered until 1613 when Rory O'Cahan, the eldest son of Sir Donnell, arrived in England. This was the year in which Lady O'Cahan arrived in London with her husband. There was a complaint made by Sir Donnell about the number of cows he had entrusted to his tenants. He left his father a prisoner in the Tower of London. Rory returned to Ireland to discover Thomas Phillips occupying his father's castle and its lands. He was confined to a freehold near the mountains. He was a youth of high spirits and he was not satisfied with the status quo. There was a campaign in 1615 in which he became one of the leading figures.

The campaign revolved around three individuals. The first campaign took place about May 1614 at the house of Gill three miles from Coleraine. There were Gills living at Macosquin and the home was almost certainly Gill's house at Donerat, near the Camus ford, and this would be a convenient meeting place. Quite a large party seems to have congregated here. From North Antrim came the MacDonnells – Alexander, Lodder, Sorley and Rice. Alexander and Sorley were the nephews of the Sir Randal MacDonnell, who held lands in the Glens of Antrim and beyond. The O'Cahans were reproached by Rory and by Gorry who had been granted a large freehold in the Coleraine barony. The O'Mullans were represented by James McBrian and by Art McJames.

The clansmen now made their way to a hilltop, consisting of Rory and Gorry O'Cahan, Alexander and Lodder MacDonnell, who were drinking beer. Alexander, Lodder and Rory now voiced their discontent with the situation – what would happen to their lands, and how they would be forced to support themselves on such a small income. They were in agreement and prepared themselves for a rising to capture some of the main towns. Everyone else was now acquainted with the plot. They took an oath in secrecy, Rory O'Cahan always carrying a book with him if such a situation should arise. Articles of agreement were drawn up between Shane McGillduffe Og O'Mullan and Rory. Articles were drawn up between all the conspirators and delivered into the custody of the MacDonnells. A letter was drawn up discussing their intentions to Brian Crossagh O'Neill, whose father was in prison. Several others were expected to join them. The letter was written by one Shane McGillduffe Oge and signed by the main conspirators then sent for good keeping to Dalton Duffe, a dwarf.

Everyone was to gather as many arms as possible as a preliminary step. The MacDonnells were to recruit men from the Isles. The attack was to start with the seizure of Coleraine. Rory O'Cahan and his friends would be drinking that day, and Rory said that the fort at Culmore would be defended. However, the town was burned when others were let in. Many other towns and forts were burned and captured – Derry, Lifford, Masserene, Charlemont, Mountjoy and Carrickfergus. No one was to be spared, except John Rowley and Sir Richard Hansard. They were held as hostages for the return of Sir Donnell O'Cahan, Sir Neill Garve O'Donnell, Sir Cormac McBrian O'Neill, and Con Gregy O'Neill (son of Tyrone) and were released into the custody of the competitors. He had been imprisoned in the fort of Charlemont. There is no mention of Sir Thomas Phillips as a hostage. Rory O'Cahan said that he would cut off his head and that he would soon, if it was necessary, be in charge of the castle at Limavady.

The plan seemed sound enough but it did not take into account the number of people of Irish birth who preferred to co-operate with Dublin Castle. In addition to this there was too much drinking and too much talk. Rory O'Cahan talked too much and he hated Sir Thomas, who had captured his father, and had occupied his castle and a considerable portion of his land. Rory was wanting in discretion but he did not control his temper outbursts in the face of Sir Thomas, who made ready an attack upon the Irish.

The entire company was in danger of collapse, and this undermined the weakness of the conspirators. It collapsed on 31 January 1615 at Cloghan in the Balteagh area. At this point Donnell O'Manus O'Mullan, about twenty-one years of age, brought his bride to his father's house. His father, Manus McGilreagh, had obtained the freehold of Cloghan at the time of the plantation and the family was on good terms with Sir Thomas Phillips. The examination of Donnell O'Mullan and the incident is recorded as follows: On the first day of January, Rory Oge O'Cahan came to the house of this despondent's father along with six men, O'Cahan being mounted on a horse, with sword by his side. One of them carried a fowling piece and had a powder bag and a bag of bullets. The other five were Tirlagh O'Mullan; McJames; Patrick Mullan McManus; McNogher and two others of the Creevies' sept; the names are not known. They came into the house, and Rory O'Doherty stood firm in his property with his firing piece. He stripped people that did not agree with him, and the examiners wanted him either to go forward to the house or else take the piece from him. O'Cahan wanted to drink his fill before entering the house.

Charles Fisher and Rice Jones, in the examination, confirmed the outline of the quarrel with Rory O'Cahan. Sir Thomas Phillips held a castle that was Rory's by right of inheritance, and he hoped to fall into possession of it again despite the English and the Scots. Fisher and James were friends of Sir Thomas Phillips and they must have reached Phillips almost immediately.

One of the main conspirators had behaved in a childish manner and ruined the company. The conspirators were sought out and arrested, and were jailed at Londonderry. They were James McBrian O'Mullan; Shane McGillduffe Oge O'Mullan. Others were jailed at Carrickfergus. On 24 April the wife of McBrian O'Mullan came in distress to Anthony Mahone's house in Newtown Limavady. She wanted to speak in confidence with Mahone. He took with him a maidservant who spoke Gaelic. He wanted to know what his visitor had said. She wanted to speak to Sir Thomas on behalf of her husband and offered him twenty cattle for his trouble. She said that her husband had been found in the company of the conspiracy and that she had advised him to keep out of trouble. There were others that had threatened to kill him if he did not consent to it and follow their orders.

A series of examinations were conducted from February onwards; three confessions were obtained and it is from these incidents that we learn the state of the situation. Torture was used – the rack – and one of those subjected to it was Cuconnaght O'Keenan, who confessed, with Davy Mullan as the interpreter. The first witness to all this was Sir Thomas Phillips, who was said to have been the prime mover in stamping out the conspiracy. Sir Thomas had a good deal to lose. O'Keenan's confession, made under torture, was open to question.

Another incident happened in May, all of which concerned the O'Mullans. They started to travel on the evening of Tuesday, 9 May from Limavady to Ballyquinn, where they expected to see Sir Thomas Phillips. Kugher McGillpatrick, about sixty years of age, made a statement to Sir Thomas on the following day when there was a quarrel between Art McTomlen and Brian McShane Boy, which ended up in blows. Art McTomlen is said to have cast up matters to Brian McShane. Brian, however, was a churchwarden, but he did not attend to his office. He had sixteen Masses said in his house, where the priest got a white cow for his services. The two McShane brothers had been sent into the Clandeboye for Neill Mclught McMurtagh O'Neill to meet Rory O'Cahan. O'Neill, however, was told to go on some other errand as a camouflage. According to the statement McTomlen said that O'Neill was not really interested in conducting business with Sir Thomas Phillips. On the way he stayed at the house of Brian and James McShane Boy. There was now a plot to seize Limavady Castle. Art McTomlen said that the two brothers were as deeply involved in conspiracy as O'Cahan was.

Knogher McGillpatrick also said that Edmund Groom McTomlen (a constable) had hoped to get Mr Babington to cut off his head. There was to be a sharing-out of goods that Babington had judicially obtained for himself and others. Mr Babington was advised to leave his house and to live under Sir Thomas Phillips in safety. William Babington had also built an inn for travellers on the road from Coleraine to Derry. Babington was soon reported to have died, but under what circumstances, natural or foul, it is hard to determine.

All the other O'Mullans were examined, who had been present at the quarrel. They consented that there was a quarrel between Art McTomlen and Brian McShane Boy, but they denied the burning of Derry. James McKnoghter and Manus McGilreagh said that they had no idea of the threats made by Edmund Groom. The clan was deeply divided in its attitude to the new regime. Some, like Donnell Mullan, were on good terms with Sir Thomas Phillips' men. Others like Murtagh and Iver Mullan had served as soldiers with Sir Thomas. On the other wing were names like Gillduffe Oge, a branch of Ballyness, who felt that revolt was an option. Gillduffe O'Mullan and his four sons, with Brian O'Mullan, are sited as having been involved in the 1615 plot and are described as desperate men. There was, however, a large number of men that chose the middle course, and said that the least said the easiest mended.

Twenty-five people were charged with high treason for taking part in the 1615 conspiracy. The grand jury included Manus O'Cahan and Cowy Ballagh McRichard O'Cahan. There were fifteen jurymen. According to the records some of the men were given notes, detailing what had happened. Some were acquitted, including James McBrian O'Mullan and Shane McGillduffe Og Mullan. Four of the men were hanged – Rorie Oge O'Cahan, Gloria McManus O'Cahan, Cuconnaught O'Keenan and Laglin O'Laverty, a priest. Several others were also hanged, but the dwarf,

Dalton Duffe, was acquitted. Alexander MacDonnell, who was also involved, also was acquitted. Some others went to the Tower of London. Religion plays a large part in the revolt and this was said to be inevitable because of the unfriendly nature of the plantation policies. It meant a change in religion, law, language and customs. The Bishop of Derry had been killed by Docwra's men in the Enagh district in their plans for the conquest of O'Cahan's country. The policies of the plantation were not often carried out. There was an investigation into the position at the close of 1631. There were twenty priests on the Skinners' estate, including Donnagh O'Cahan, Shane O'Cahan and Fardoragh O'Cahan. Evidence was given by Cormach O'Mullan that Richard Kirby, sheriff of the town in County Londonderry, had entertained four separate pleas in his court against people for not paying their priest's fees. The priest had excommunicated them for four and a half years. There were also wandering friars that lived off the countryside, one of which was Gillegrome McTeige, which is likely the name given as Gillecome McTeig, mentioned in the quarrels between the two O'Mullans.

The 1615 conspiracy was only in the planning stages, but there is plenty of evidence that a conspiracy was on the agenda. Rory O'Cahan hated Sir Thomas and wanted to kill him and repossess the O'Cahan lands. There was sufficient reason for this action. But through his own incompetence, he lost his life and possession of the freehold granted to Sir Donnell's son. Lady O'Cahan seems to have continued in the other sector of the freehold with her other son, Donnell. In 1617 Cormac O'Mullan and some other individuals of standing were put in charge of her lands. Some let their freeholds as a result of the role they played in the conspiracy.

Between 1615 and the Irish Rebellion of 1641 some of the O'Cahans went to Europe. Brian O'Haggan, examined in February 1627, explains how he brought from Europe letters quilted in the belly pieces of his doublet. He described how he brought one from Donnell Beleach McManus O'Cahan to his father Manus O'Cahan, living within two miles of Londonderry, together with his brother Brian McManus. He handed over the message in a pub at the ferry of Derry. He said that Brian O'Cahan went to England and eventually to the Low Countries. This seems to refer to Captain McManus O'Cahan and his son. Manus had received the most fertile freehold given to any Gael in County Derry.

Sir Donnell had a younger son – Sir Donnell – and the hopes of the O'Cahan centred around him. This Donnell has sometimes been known as Donnell Oge (Donnell the Younger) because he was born while Donnell Geimhleach (Donnell of Feather) was in jail with her jailed husband. He went abroad to learn about warfare, and spent many years in Europe.

Alice Milligan wrote a famous poem about him:

There is not one left
No home at Enagh or Faughan Vale, not cattle in Glenconchkeine;
No ship on the wide reaches of the lough to sail o'er the Scottish Sea,
And the son of chiefs in the land of his sire is a homeless Rapparee.

# Chapter 10

## *The Clans Revolt*

The year 1641 was noted for the settlers who had been surviving in a struggle against natural and political forces. The rebellion broke out at the close of the year. Land had been confiscated; there was the plantation and the proscribing of the Roman Catholic faith. James MacDonnell, a leader in the revolt in North Antrim said that he did not wish to usurp the authority of the Crown. Their only hope was that they could worship in peace their Catholic faith and for everyone to enjoy their inheritance.

Sir Phelim O'Neill was leader of the revolt in Ulster, and he was fixed to usurp a position in the colonization on a date put at 23 October 1641. It was a Sunday and he was fixed to seize positions of importance throughout the province. O'Hagan and others surprised their castle, despoiling the British settlers of their goods. The insurgents seized Desertmartin and Magherafelt, and eventually burned them both. The whole barony of Loughinsolin was overrun. Coleraine had been warned of a rising. Mr William Rowley was present at the siege of Moneymore on a Saturday afternoon. He fled to Coleraine, where he arrived at about eight o'clock on Sunday morning. A great number of religious fled to Coleraine throughout that day. There was early intelligence about the revolt at Coleraine, and on the same Sunday he rode on horseback to Derrykeighan Church, where the congregation was told of the great happenings of the previous day. Captain William McPhedris of Loughgiel had the task of taking Dunluce Castle, lest it be captured by the Gaelic rebels. At this time the Earl of Antrim was absent from Dublin. Captain McPhedris and a dozen armed men with swords and pistols rode forth to Dunluce and warned the scots in the town, but they did not gain entrance to the castle, which was held by one Captain Digby, on Antrim's behalf. Dunluce remained in a state of armed neutrality, which lasted throughout the coming winter. Stewart also placed garrisons, composed mainly of Scots, in the house and church at Ballintoy and at various other key positions throughout the north.

Sir Phelim O'Neill had seized the forts of Mountjoy and Charlemont, and the town of Dungiven. Counties Cavan and Monaghan were overrun by the O'Reillys and Maguires. In the south, Owen O'Connolly from Moneymore had warned Dublin Castle about the delicate situation in Ulster. As a result there was no revolt in the area for a while.

The rebellion at Londonderry had been mainly confined to the Barony of Loughinsolin in South Derry, and Ballycastle was securely held. Dungiven Castle was entrusted to Manus McCowy Ballagh McRichard who was granted the freehold in the parish of Bovevagh near Dungiven. This Manus was believed to be a 'Castle Catholic', but it is said that he had betrayed his trust. He had now turned rebel, and he became one of the most cruel and bloody villains of the time. In the Coleraine barony 250 men were placed at Garvagh where they were attacked by a great force. Many were killed and were forced to retreat. The area from Coleraine to Aghadowey and Garvagh seems to have been settled with colonizers as usual. On 16 November it was reported to the Irish House of Commons that the insurgents were not to come to Coleraine nor within six or seven miles of it.

The position changed very rapidly. Peter Gates, having property at Ballykelly, who was a Roman Catholic, stated that James Farrell of that townland was promised protection from the English, who were his neighbours, to induce him to stay in Ulster. About 21 November, Farrell and some followers attacked the English settlers; a number of them were killed. Amongst the rebels were Brian McGillan and two or three of his sons. The O'Mullans were also sited as rebels. There was Shane Roe O'Mullan and other O'Mullans, including Shane McGillduff Oge and Art McGillduffe Oge. The colonizers' houses were burned and the cattle and goods taken.

Revolt proceeded on a large scale. A large Irish force of about 1,800 men approached Garvagh on 13 December and were met by the Garvagh garrison at Revelyn Hill. However, the Garvagh forces were greatly outnumbered and suffered a resounding defeat. Edmund Rowley and William Canning (who was in charge) were both killed with their officers and about 200 men. John Stockman, a tanner, and his wife, Mary, lived in a house near Desertoghill. Their house was below the hill where the battle took place. Mary Stockman later told William Taffe, a lieutenant colonel in the insurgent forces that Rory Ballagh O'Cahan arrived in the evening of the day on which the battle was fought. They demanded the keys of the church, saying that some English had fled to it and were there at the present moment. Mrs Stockman replied that she did not have the keys; at this they departed. At the time of the Ordnance Survey, it was recorded that the Protestants had retreated to the old church at Desertoghill. Here they were all killed.

After the defeat at Garvagh the colonists at Aghadowey fled to Coleraine. John Hill's house was burned together with other houses, described as being in the vicinity near Sunday's well in the marshes of the parish of Coleraine, Dunboe and Macosquin. This rising engulfed the entire country, which was described as being burned up to the region of the river Foyle. The rebels met the men of Derry at the ferry. Coleraine was now the sole refuge in the Barony of Coleraine. About twenty persons had found refuge in the town. The house at Coleraine was filled up as well as the church. Little huts had been built – the churchyard was packed with the poor. The outer walls of the town had been improved after much labour to present a reasonable defence. There were about 650 men in the town of Coleraine, commanded and paid for weekly by nine captains. The highest paid made up a force of one hundred men. There were 500 men in the town who had no weapons. The Mayor of Coleraine wrote to Dublin in the middle of January asking for money to pay the soldiers' and for arms and food. They said that the town was full up and that there was no room for additional companies and private citizens. They sent 3,000 women and children to Scotland from the port of Coleraine, so that the remainder of the garrison could hold out with the reduction of food supplies. A troop of one hundred cavalry was also raised to make incursions into the countryside.

Catholic forces under Captain Burlaees' company were disarmed – they were mostly Roman Catholic. There was some question of loyalty by those who had hitherto been subject to the Crown. As the 1641 Rebellion gathered momentun, the old saying was that nothing succeeds like success. There were those that at first did not like the idea of an uprising, and were tempted to join hands with those who seemed to be heading for success. There was the case of the Scots Highlanders in North Antrim, whose leading family was the MacDonnells; their head was the Earl of Antrim, who lived in the southern part of the Glens. Archibald Stewart of Ballintoy managed to raise a regiment of nearly 800 men from amongst his own tenantry and the Earl of Antrim's tenants. He decided to pursue a policy that would dislodge the Earl of Antrim from his position in the rebellion. He appointed his own cousin, Alister MacCollkittagh MacDonnell, a good foot soldier, to be one of the captains of the regiment and to command a company of Highlanders – this proved later to have been a serious mistake.

Stewart's regiment lay at Portna, near Kilrea, so that he could capture Bannside. Across the river Bann lay the isolated strongpoint of Agivey Castle besieged by a force of 500 men, under the command of Manus

Roe O'Cahan. The regiment was all British and were detailed to convey Mr George Canning and his men safely across the river from Agivey Castle. The Gaels and the Scots Highlanders in the regiment did not follow, and were pursued by Alister MacCollkittagh and James McColl MacDonnell so that they could attack the British troops. The Irish and the Highlanders rose two hours before dawn and surprised some of the British in their beds. They surrounded and shot others who had headed the clan. This has gone down in history as the Portna Massacre, on Monday, 3 January 1642.

This was the signal for a general revolt of Gaels and Highlanders in North Antrim. MacDonnell and McAlister were joined by the O'Hagans, led by one John Mortimer with five regiments from County Derry, and later by the McMullans and others. There was an orgy of destruction in the Route, carried out by a mixed force, and this was more extreme than on any other occasion. James McColl MacDonnell marched from his house near Bannside and burned a village called the Coss. He then proceeded to Ballymoney where they killed any British left and burned the town. Now they headed for the strongpoint of Ballintoy through the parishes of Derrykeighan and Billy. This encouraged a rising by those who had rebel sympathies. At Carnkerrin in Derrykeighan Parish a number of settlers heading for Ballintoy were trapped and killed by Toole McAllister and others who lived in the vicinity. In the parish of Billy Mrs Jennett Neaven saw the rebels advancing, led by John Mortimer riding a black horse. Many of her relations were put to death, and she herself fled with her child and another woman into the moss. Here they lay hidden for two nights and two days. Overrun by hunger they ventured forth in search of sustenance.

The rebels attacked Ballintoy House and they marched along the coast to Dunluce; they bedded down at Ballymagary. Captain Rigby, who held the castle for the Earl of Antrim, was asked to surrender it, but he refused. As a result the town of Dunluce was burnt. The next day they marched back to Derrykeighan, where a proclamation was made that any using the English language should be hanged. Mrs Neaven said that she had gone to Derrykeighan after leaving the moss and had learned from the Highlanders and Irish about the death of her brother. They now proceeded to Oldstone Castle, which was surrendered on 16 January, which brought to an end the rebellion in the Route.

The second week of January came about. The full seriousness of the situation was realized at both Derry and Coleraine. The leadership of the MacDonnells in the rebellion had greatly troubled the situation in North Antrim. Those successful rebels received further aid. The men of Rathlin Island had helped to make up the MacDonnell forces of over

2,000 men. Tirlagh O'Neill had devastated South Antrim, and now advanced north towards Coleraine. Between Coleraine and Carrickfergus lay two or three strongpoints. Coleraine was overcrowded as a result of Archibald Stewart's withdrawal into the town in fear of the rebels. The regiment was only numbered at 300 to 400 men.

Carrickfergus Castle was the only important fort that the British Forces held in County Antrim. On the other side of Coleraine, Derry was of most importance. The castles of Dungiven, Ballycastle and Limavady were intact as the rebellion gathered strength. The Mayor of Londonderry wrote to the Lords Justices in Dublin on 10 January, letting them know about their shortage of ammunition and powder. They said that missiles daily threatened them, and there were so many people confined within the city. They said that if they escaped from the enemy, hunger would overcome them as well as all kinds of sicknesses. The shipping carried people to Scotland, using all the ships that the city possessed. The terrors of the rebellion had struck fear into the hearts of the British. On the same day, 10 January 1642, James MacDonnell wrote to Archibald Stewart, demanding the surrender of Coleraine. If this were done, boats would be sent from Rathlin Island to Portrush to embark the Scots people. He assured them that if they surrendered all the forces in the countryside, they would be safe. There were also other regiments across the Bann that had been pillaging. Women were killed and some people were hung. Old people of over sixty were also killed.

There were many excuses for the 1641 Rebellion. However, some of the lives of the women and children were respected. The insurrection could be compared to Mountjoy's conquest of Ulster. The official policy was the devastation of the land, so farmers were put to death with all the rest.

As a result of James MacDonnell's letter, the Mayor of Coleraine wrote to the Lords Justices about it. In it they mentioned their great need of assistance, and they said that their resolution was to fight until the end. A little while later they went over to the offensive against the rebel troops, whose headquarters were at Ballymoney. Archibald marched from Coleraine in the direction of the town. He wanted to incite the enemy into battle. He was met at the Laney by a force similar in size to his own, commanded by experienced soldiers. Alister MacDonnell had no cavalry of his own; he managed to entice Stewart's horse into a bog. MacDonnell's men fired a single shot from their muskets and attacked the enemy with sword in hand. The Highland force was formidable – Stewart's men were routed and most of them were killed. Friday, 18 February has become known amongst the British as 'Black Friday'.

Coleraine was secure now that the troops had surrounded the town.

Their headquarters was to be at Ballyrashane, where the camp was at Peter Lowry's and the Stirling houses. Lowry had his own force. The camp lay in a fold in the hills from Ballyversal into Kiswatty and Knockinkerragh. Across the river Bann the position was held by O'Cahan, who held Agivey Castle. He was lieutenant colonel to Manus Roe O'Cahan. Roe was also in rebel hands and was a great obstacle to the garrison at Coleraine since it commanded the fishing. In the parish of Dunboe, Creeney Oge O'Cahan of Milligan took up his residence at Thomas Haslett's house.

Foraging parties were sent forth from Coleraine into the surrounding countryside, but they were liable to be cut off. Donnaghy O'Cahan of Killowen told later how these parties had set out in a foraging expedition west of the river Bann on Saint Patrick's Day, 1642. The rebels saw one party come out of a stockyard. They armed themselves and made their retreat to the Bann; Donnaghy O'Cahan and three other soldiers, making up a second party, were cut off by some of Creeney Oge O'Cahan's men. They got between them and the Bann, forcing them to surrender, and were sent as prisoners to Creeney Oge's headquarters at Dunboe. They were later transferred to Agivey Castle.

The fever at Coleraine had now lasted four months, having started in the spring. A number who lived at Coleraine during the 1641 Rebellion said that an account kept by a gentleman called Henry Beresford, claimed that 100–150 persons died weekly, making a total of about 2,000. The dead were buried in vast and wide holes. They were buried, packed like herrings. Now the Earl of Antrim travelled north from Dublin to Dunluce in April. He persuaded Alister MacDonnell to raise the siege of Coleraine so that the people could graze their cattle within a circuit of three miles around the town. The Earl of Antrim also sent sixty loads of corn and one hundred fat cattle.

The situation at Limavady was also very different. Sir Thomas Phillips, who had been at loggerheads with the London companies, had died a few years before the rebellion. Their names – Dudley and Thomas – headed a petition dated 21 March 1642, and they sent it to the Lords Justices and Council in Dublin. There were other names that were mentioned. Sir John McClelland of Galloway built a castle at Ballycastle on the Haberdashers' estate, which he controlled for the Londoners. He brought over several kinsmen and other Scots colonizers to the Roe Valley.

The country was the richest and best placed in the whole of Londonderry, but the petition showed that it had fallen into a most miserable and lamentable state. The settlers were murdered almost daily and the wives and children stripped. The better sort fled to Coleraine and Londonderry, a refuge from the Catholic rebels. The remainder were hemmed up in two castles in the heart of the county. The road between Derry and Coleraine was well armed, and also between Coleraine and Ballycastle, where there were two castles, containing about 1,000 men, women and children and 300 fighting men. It was dangerous to travel between the castles without a guard or to fetch water in the event of enemy fire. They said that they were short of victuals, eating one meal a day. They were forced to sally forth sometimes, and they had left twenty men and slew about one hundred. The women and children ate up most of the stores.

Another petition was sent to Dudley Phillips, saying that he had maintained some men since the beginning of the rebellion. Three hundred men at Limavady were at his own charge, but there was nothing left to support his troops. He requested that he and his brethren be given commission to command 300 foot and one troop of horse, and he also requested arms, ammunition and pay for the soldiers. The first petition begged for ointments as they had many wounded men. Phillips said that he had despatched some men for the rebels at Ballycastle, which was in a worse condition than Limavady. At Ballycastle there were about 120 men, half of them naked and without weapons. Dudley Phillips was sent two barrels of powder, forty barrels of herrings and twelve barrels of beef from Dublin. It was hoped that Londonderry would hold out until supplies arrived.

There was now in the next few months a turning point in the rebellion. On 15 April a relieving Scots army landed at Carrickfergus. Coleraine had been relieved by the Laggan forces. These forces had been raised from settlers in East Donegal, and were commanded by professional soldiers – i.e. Sir William and Sir Robert Stewart. They took the castle at Strabane, and made a foray into County Londonderry. Near the city they were joined by four companies from Londonderry. They marched on Limavady. This was a most intensive campaign and is described in two letters from Sir Robert and Sir William and in a pamphlet by Colonel Audley Mervyn, one of their officers. It is now possible to reconstruct the movements of the forces.

The Laggan troops marched forth to Limavady and Ballycastle. Captain Thomas Phillips was in command at Limavady. His elder brother, Dudley Phillips, had gone with three boats to bring food to Derry. The troops were a sight for sore eyes, and were welcome at the two castles, where the people had given up hope of relief. Now they marched forth to Magilligan, where they met with scattered small parties of the insurgents, each numbering twenty or thirty. They had killed about 200 of them. They reached Benevenagh and came as far as Articlare, having heard about the state of Coleraine.

They were determined to bring relief to the town. Instead they changed direction towards the hills and made for Dungiven. They may have been encamped at Ardmore, where the field between the old castle of Ardmore and the ancient church of Balteagh was known as Camp Hill.

The Irish forces had learned of the attack by the Lagganers and had gathered in strength to oppose them. This was O'Cahan's territory, and would not be yielded without a struggle. There were a large number of troops, ranging in number from Coll Shane O'Cahan, 300 men; Bryan McArt Oge, 500 men; Con O'Gormley, one hundred men. The date of the battle that took place between Limavady Castle and Dungiven has been put at Tuesday, 7 May. The position is given as two and a half miles from Dungiven and four and a half miles from Newtown Limavady, and a quarter of a mile east of the road leading from one town to another. One of the forces is said to have been stationed north-east of the Roe on a farm occupied by one Joseph Fleming in the townland of Gortaclave.

Ulster was now in a state of war with itself. Men were sworn to fight until the last man. The rebels were drawn up in good order and had the advantage of sun and wind. The soldiers were ready to charge and Sir William Stewart had never experienced such a band of men. The charging soldiers were met with by a volley from eighty musketeers, who returned the fire with the support of their troops. The first assault had attacked the Laggan forces. They counter-attacked and broke their opponents' lines. The Irish/Gaelic force now retreated and were pursued in all directions for about two miles until the ground became rough, so it was hard to follow. The Gaelic forces lost nine of their colours.

Artillery may have been used, since metal balls 7–10 pounds in weight were found in the area many years later. When the Ordnance Survey inspectors visited the area they noted anything that might be connected with the battle. They visited the holding of Joseph Stirling in Gorticlare. Weapons lay 6–12 inches above the ground. Thomas McClelland was an officer in one of the rebel armies. A severe battle was fought in which many died, amongst them Robert McClelland. Other soldiers were buried in humble graves without any ceremony to remember them. Lieutenant McClelland remembered the spot where his brother Thomas was buried, and a stone was procured. A white stone was placed at the head of the grave. In the following year ploughing raised the ground around the stone. Moss grew over the grave, but the area of the battleground is remembered to this day.

They were also shown a spot within thirty perches of the road leading from Garvagh on Jacob Smyth's holding in Mulkeeragh. His father, Isach, died, and Jacob was cutting the bog at this spot in the summer of 1753 when he found a dead body stretched at full length. The body was in a uniform of tartan, with a large tartan cloak above it. Both garment and body were well preserved. The finding of the body was quite an occasion for the locals, and people went to see it. An inquest was held and the body was reinterred. It is thought that the body was one of the victims of the 1641 Rebellion. Doubts can be raised about identification. The grave bears the inscription date 1641 rather than 1642.

Sir William Stewart wrote a letter setting out the sequel of the battle. He said that they then drew their men together and were marching on Dungiven Castle. Manus McQuay Ballagh O'Cahan, who had fled out of the field, sent Mr Dudley Phillips, who with his horse had performed good services. He said that he wished to parley with him. This he accepted and in conclusion agreed with Manus that they should subject themselves to the King's mercy. He was to render up his castle, and the party agreed, rather than the taking of it by force, which would mean loss of men and that many British men and women would be destroyed within it. Manus and the rest were sent as prisoners to Londonderry. On the way they destroyed all the corn that was thought to aid the rebels.

Early in the letter the Keeper of Dungiven Castle is referred to as Lieutenant Colonel Manus McQuay, who held from the King 2,000 acres freehold. It was later said that Lieutenant Colonel O'Cahan had been entrusted with the keeping of Dungiven Castle by Sir John Vaughan, the military commander at Londonderry. He said that O'Cahan had betrayed a trust. He crossed sides and was a thorough villain. This Manus was the son of Coyne Ballagh or Cowy Ballagh McRichard O'Cahan. He had surrendered Dungiven Castle to Docwra just over twenty years previously on 20 April 1602. These O'Cahans shifted their theatre of operations to the parish of Bovagh.

The Laggan forces fell heir to a large number of cattle, some of which were the property of the settlers in the Coleraine area. The troops now marched with their booty to Coleraine. They restored any cattle to their rightful owner and bestowed some as a gift to the town. They sold the rest at competitive rates. Castle Roe, which commanded the river Bann fisheries, was also seized, and authorities differ upon how much this mattered. The commander at Coleraine started to set up a garrison at Castle Roe, which was a great relief and a safeguard for the town. Having completed their tasks, the forces returned to Donegal.

A battle was fought at Gelvin, the greatest led by the O'Cahans for a generation. This persistent marshalling of the clans was necessary for fighting the English. Donnell Geimhleach of the Fetters was the surviving son of the last chief of the clan, Sir Donnell Ballagh. The O'Mullans of the local friary arrived from Spain and were joined by Sir Phelim at

Charlemont on 1 May 1642. Sir Robert later noted his arrival and said that he had come from Spain after many years of travel abroad. Two months previously Sir Arthur Hopkin from Spain gave the description of a man whose treachery he had caught wind of. He had in his company a priest, Denis Burke, of the low march, who was about thirty years of age. The person opting for leadership at Madrid is likely to have been Donnell Geimhleach, but it could have been some other O'Cahan in the service of Spain. The close coincidence of dates, the interest taken in the men and his pensioners, and those of the name O'Cahan, all point to the importance of Donnell Geimhleach.

The Scots forces marched under Monro north through County Antrim, and by 18 June had encamped at Ballymoney. Here they attended to the surrounding countryside, the insurgent army which had been blockading Coleraine having crossed the river Roe, and under Alister MacDonnell joined Sir Phelim O'Neill's forces. Monro laid siege to Dunluce Castle, and the Earl of Antrim surrendered it and himself. Five hundred men arrived at the river Bann at Canning's Ferry, and Colonel Clothsworthy took a troop of horse to Coleraine. Antrim set out for Ballymoney, heading for the mouth of the Bann, where there was a fort called McNaghten's Fort about two miles from Ballymoney. It was said that Ballymoney was in the middle of a bog but very strong, and here the McNaghtens owned lands. The high ground where the Irish had encamped overlooked Coleraine. Coleraine was at this time also bogland. Now the landlord, the Earl of Antrim, surrendered to a force under Captain Connolly, who had let the women and children go. The men were put at one hundred and were escorted by them to the main encampment at Dunmull near Bally-Beardiviville. They were accused of having taken part in the rebellion, and about fifteen to twenty were put to death, this being generally called the Dunmull Massacre.

On the other side of the river Bann, following the attack by the Laggan forces, the Gaels burned Movangher and Agivey Castles, and Ferdonough O'Cahan's men took to the woods. It was dangerous countryside, especially in summer. About January a small group of three men had travelled from Coleraine to Aghadowey to see what had befallen their houses and goods there, which they had abandoned. During their search they were surprised by twelve Irish horsemen, and fled into the bogland. They were pursued and taken prisoner, except a man who had made off in a different direction. The men were poorly treated. The Gaels wanted some of the women put to death, but others said that they had no orders to kill women.

The main body of the troops in the Coleraine vicinity hitched up with Sir Phelim O'Neill's forces. They marched into Donegal in order to attack the Laggan forces. They were still accompanied by the four forces of companies from Derry and a force of sixty horsemen under Captain Phillips. They were the same troops that had won a victory at Gelvin. Gaelic and English forces clashed at Glenmaquin on 16 June 1642. The Laggan forces were again victorious. Captain Dudley Phillips, who had left one hundred men at Limavady Castle, under command of his brother Thomas Alister MacDonnell, on the Catholic side, had led a fierce attack on Sir Robert Stewart's brigade. He was shot and seriously wounded. Donnell O'Cahan managed to bring the wounded to safety on a litter.

The Irish forces were luckier in the summer. Donnell O'Cahan confronted a large body of Scots at Vow Ferry on the Bann on 16 August. O'Cahan defeated the Scots, who had lost 150 men; they took to the forests. On the 29th of the month a great council was held of the nobles in Ulster, including the O'Cahans, who were based at Clones. Sir Phelim resigned the leadership of the rebels in Ulster in favour of Owen Roe O'Neill, who had arrived from the Continent. Owen Roe O'Neill's grandfather was a brother of Shane O'Neill or Shane the Proud. Owen was therefore a nephew of the famous Red Hugh O'Neill of Tyrone. Owen Roe was well suited for the task which he now set out to accomplish and he had a high standard of honour. He believed in strict discipline as the troops observed him in action. The poor Gaels had suffered badly as a result of internal wars. In O'Mullan's diary for 8 September 1642, he tells how O'Cahan apportioned pay for the two sons of Collkittagh-Gillespie and Randal. Twenty-five pounds was now granted towards buying clothing, and coigny on his own (O'Cahan's) creaghts. A general muster was announced and the rebels were instructed to carry away from the Gaels the people of every home who had coigny, their cows and horses together with their sheep and goats. They now brought the plunder to the Coleraine area. Here they raised a fortification for themselves.

In the following year the O'Cahans lost many of their most important men. One of the O'Cahans was killed in December 1642. A more serious loss took place in the following spring; here there was a force of 3,000 men under Sir Robert Stewart situated as far as Clossagh Trwagh. O'Mullan wrote a vivid description of events.

Largy had received five of their horsemen. Sir Phelim O'Neill and O'Kane happened to be near the place with one hundred men and one hundred foot. The enemy was sized up and they saw the five horsemen near him. O'Kane placed himself between the two forces, but his horse fell with him. The horse's head was hurt, and O'Kane found it impossible to get him on his feet. He was taken prisoner immediately and the horsemen were able to retreat in safety from the enemy. Sir Phelim said that he would not expect them to carry off O'Kane. He set out in pursuit and a Scots trooper sent a bullet through O'Kane's head. They carried away his horse and weapons. Sir Phelim had the body buried at Armagh. Thus ended a phase in this unfortunate family's history, but at least his death was a quick one unlike that of his brother, condemned and hanged in 1615, or his father who died in the Tower of London after many years of confinement. Many years later a seal of the Spanish style and workmanship was uncovered in County Londonderry and was attributed to Donnell O'Cahan. The seal had been preserved in Dublin by a Major Cane. An engraving of the impression of the seal was preserved by the officers of the Ordnance Survey, but the position of the page on which it appeared had been cut off. There is a lasting memorial in the name 'Donald's Hill'.

The end to civil war came in September 1643. In the following year Alister MacDonnell went with an army of soldiers from Scotland to fight for Montrose against the Covenanters. Captain Thomas O'Cahan was in their number. He distinguished himself at a battle at Fyvie, but he was executed in Edinburgh after the Battle of Philiphaugh, fought on 13 September 1645. He may have belonged to the O'Cahans of Dunseverick. There were more O'Cahan's losses in 1645. Fifteen thousand Ulstermen served under the Earl of Castlehaven, who was appointed in command of the Confederate Irish forces. He took the fort of Lismore from Captain Manus Ballagh McRicard O'Cahan. Manus had surrendered Dungiven Castle to the Lagganers. He may have escaped from his captors. Both Manus and his brother were in service in the 1641 Rebellion, according to the state papers. O'Mullan recorded that on 7 March, the Enniskillen men attacked and plundered many landowners, including the daughter of Cooey Ballagh McRichard. The last captain killed at the spot was a son of Captain Manus, who had received a substantial freehold near Derry. He became known as Manus the Anglicized.

The O'Cahans were again cited in the rebellion. In 1646 Shane and Richard O'Kane, with 3,000 men, burned Dunseverick. In January Shane O'Kane, with 3,000 men, attacked the garrison at Kells where Colonel Theophilus Jones was stationed with 300 men. They went at a gallop towards Kells. The foot soldiers scaled the walls whilst the cavalry remained outside. One hundred and thirty of Colonel Jones's men asked to be spared and given quarter. Upwards of 200 were killed.

King Charles I was executed in 1649; Cromwell assumed supreme power. A questionable situation now arose in Ireland, for there were the Irish insurgents contending for their own ends – the Royalist who wanted revenge for Charles's death and those who supported Cromwell and Parliament. In 1649 Owen Roe O'Neill, said to have been the best general that the Gaels ever had, became sick and died. The Royalists and the

Gaels joined forces and appointed Heber McMahon, the Bishop of Clogher, as their general. Coote was the commander-in-chief of the Republican and Parliamentary forces in Ulster. His main strength lay in the north-west, and at Londonderry. McMahon invaded County Londonderry, where he laid siege to Dungiven Castle, held by Lieutenant Michael Beresford. It was gallantly defended, but it was taken by storm. Ballycastle, in Aghanloo district, was surrendered. The situation at Limavady was also to prove sticky. Major Phillips burned his outhouses or anything that might aid the enemy. On 21 June 1650 the Republican forces met at Schear-Saullis, two miles south-west of Letterkenny. This was the last battle to be fought on Ulster soil until the revolution, and it was contested for some time. On the Gaelic side, Major General Shane O'Cahan was killed. He was known as Shane of Brackfield. One of the officers killed at Schaer-Saullis was Captain James Mullan.

The prolonged struggle since 1641 had disastrous effects upon the colonization. It was reported that the Ironmongers' manor, the castle and all other buildings, together with the church, the corn mill and three bridges had been totally destroyed in the rebellion. Timber had been greatly wasted so there were now only twenty timber trees fit for building on the entire estate.

Regarding the wars of rebellion, it is useful to turn to the situation at Derry, Limavady and Coleraine. At the close of 1688 the Earl of Antrim's forces (Catholic) were refused admission to Londonderry (Protestant). The forces arrived at Newtown Limavady on 6 December, followed by a crowd of women and children. The people of Londonderry were alarmed at their predicament. George Phillips, son of Captain Dudley Phillips of plantation fame, had become a very old man, living at a lodge which was beside the present marketplace. Derry was worried about the Catholic forces, and the Apprentice Boys took the law into their own hands and closed the gates in the face of the Earl of Antrim. An army was dispatched from Dublin to relieve the situation at Londonderry, and it arrived before Coleraine on 27 March 1689. Coleraine's fortifications consisted of a mud wall and a deep wet ditch surrounding the Protestants on three sides. The fourth side was shielded by the river Bann, which boasted a drawbridge. They marched up with five pieces of cannon. Other weapons were planted against King's Gate, attended by a body of horse and foot. They fired hotly at each other. There were many bridges and gardens near the works, but the enemy's foot attacked. There was a watermill near the town, where about thirty or forty of the grenadiers attacked the town. The attack lasted until night. The attackers were made up of a body of cavalry drawn up on a hill near the town. They withdrew their foot under cover of a snow shower, followed by their horsemen. The

Jacobite forces arrived at the Bann at Portglenone a few days later. The forces at Coleraine destroyed the bridge across the river and retreated towards Londonderry.

Despite the losses of the 1641 Rebellion there were still some O'Cahans left to take the Gaelic side. A Roger O'Cahan of Donegal seems to have raised a regiment of foot at an early date. In Colonel Cormac O'Neill of Kilmacevet's regiment were Captain Thomas O'Kane, Captain Roger O'Cahan, Lieutenant Bryan O'Kane, Ensign Darby O'Cahan and Lieutenant Richard Kane, who served in all the forces; it included Colonel Gordon O'Neill, who was the son of Sir Phelim O'Neill of 1641 fame. The major losses of clan lands and property took place at an early date. It is useful now to take a look at what had happened to the Gaelic freeholds created in the plantation/colonization period.

# Chapter 11

## *The Native Freeholders*

There were considerable grants of land during the plantation to Irish freeholders. The smaller freeholders occupied land in what is now a modern townland. The five large freeholders had considerable amounts of land. History tells several stories about the fate of these freeholders. They may have been lost by trickery and foolish bargains. One tradition in the OS Memoirs tells how an O'Cahan near Derry had several townlands. He bargained with a Mr Skipton, an Englishman, to build a house upon one of them. He was permitted to choose a townland for himself. Skipton did so, but he decided to stay in the townland, and his home was always occupied. The same story is told in a different way in an OS letter. O'Cahan is identified as Captain Manus of Brackfield, called Manus Gallda because he spoke English and had an English castle erected upon his lands. O'Cahan took advantage of him and beheaded him, and then took possession of his castle. He was not able to enjoy the fruits of victory, and the O'Cahans were defeated and sent out of Ireland.

There are many sources by which the clans and townlands can be identified. From them we can learn the major factors through which lands were lost. An important consideration was the position of the freeholders.

The largest freehold was given to Captain Manus. The freehold was nearest to Derry, some of which was sold off by Manus and his son, Bryan. The townlands, all but one in the parish of Faughanvale, remained in the estate of Shane O'Cahan, Esq. His mansion was in the townlands. Mrs Barbara Luthun claimed to draw rent from these lands, at a rent charge of £4 set up by three deeds between 1634 and 1639. Henry Thompson claimed a third of three of these lands. Hugh Thompson had paid to Shane O'Cahan a rent charge of £7 per annum for twenty-one years. If the townlands were not looked after, one third of the three townlands were to pass to Hugh Thompson or his heirs.

Shane O'Cahan was the son of Captain Manus, and was widely known as Shane of Brackfield. He played a leading role in the 1641 Rebellion and became a major general. He was slain in a battlefield near Letterkenny in 1650. His lands are marked as forfeited to the Civil Survey, and the ten townlands were assigned by the Commissioners of the Commonwealth to Lieutenant Colonel Tristram Beresford. Bryan O'Cahan also forfeited his land in the Glendermott parish. There were perhaps three other sons of Captain Manus: Cooey (killed in 1645); Richard and Donnell Ballagh. A William O'Kane, a footman of a bleach green in Cavanvegh (died in 1820, aged eighty) was said to have been a descendant of the O'Kanes of Brackfield.

Next came the freehold of Lady O'Cahan and her son, Rory. Donnell's freehold was confiscated as a result of the 1615 conspiracy. It was let for life to George Carey, the recorder of Londonderry. However, even after Donnell's departure for Europe. Lady O'Cahan remained in possession of a large portion. About 1640, in a claim by Stone, Freeman and Beresford for some portions of the Haberdashers' lands, it was recorded that Mr Beresford had obtained a lease of thirty-one years of five townlands after Lady O'Cahan's communication with the King. In 1649 there was a petition to James by Francis O'Cahan showing that King James gave O'Donnell O'Cahan, son of Sir Donnell, 1,000 acres. The petition said that he was one of the first to withdraw from the Earl of Tyrone. He said that he had served the King well; also he asked that the lands should pass to Honora, with the death of Donnell.

The Duchess of Buckingham, who married the Earl of Antrim, travelled through Limavady to visit Lady O'Cahan. It was said that she discovered Lady O'Cahan with a blanket covering her and crouched over a fire of sticks. She was reputed to have been found in a ruined castle, the windows stuffed with straw.

The third freehold was that of the O'Cahan of Dungiven. Cowey Ballagh McRichard O'Cahan was the son of Richard of Colryan and Dungiven and a grandson of Donnell the Cleric. His family has often been confused with that of Manus McCowey Ballach whose lands lay in the Coleraine barony. The key feature was the 'McRichard'. Docwra recorded the surrender of Dungiven Castle and McRichard was endowed with the large freehold generally known as Ballymacloskey, lying in the parish of Bovevagh and west of the river Roe. He claimed ten acres of land in Enish Conohor. He said that the river Roe had altered its course and left the parish on the wrong side of it. He was busy ploughing and building cabins on this piece of land in order to remain in possession of the river. Cowey Ballagh McRichard died in July 1637, and an order was made for the Parliamentary Commissioners authorizing Robert Thorton, Mayor of Londonderry, to take possession of Ballymacloskey, formerly belonging to Manus McCowey Ballagh McRichard O'Cahan; also his brethren who were in open rebellion. In the civil survey Lieutenant Colonel Tristram Beresford and Major George Carey claimed that O'Cahan had granted their fathers these townlands in return for £200 given to him. McRichard's freeholders eventually passed to George Carey of Derryard, who died in 1719. He was buried in Dungiven Priory. Captain Arthur Carey, his son, succeeded him, and in his time the property gathered debts. The property eventually passed to Henry Carey of Dungiven.

Cowey Ballagh McRichard O'Cahan lived in the townland of Flanders during his possession of the Ballymacloskey freehold. Here there was an ancient castle demolished by the McSparran family about 1803. It was said to be one of the most extensive buildings in this part of the country. The walls were built of freestone while the ground and cellar floors were of blue clay. There were many walks covered at the time of demolition with a ground bed of earth. A short distance from the front of the castle, there was a square piece supposed to have been built for the amusement of the tenants. The castle had windows. Within a short distance of it there were smaller ruins on the holding of Mamilton Connor. The construction was round and it became known as the round house. The genealogy of the Cooey Ballagh Richard family is recorded, as well as an additional piece in the Ordnance Survey for the Dungiven parish. In 1834 when one Donevan examined County Londonderry, the only person of the name of O'Kane in the county was George O'Kane. His pedigree could be traced back to Donnell the Cleric, who was the gardener to Francis Bruce of Downhill. The Careys of Derryard also lived in an ancient castle on a pretty, elevated site, in view of the river Roe and within a short distance of Pellipar House. It was seventy-two feet long and twenty-four feet broad with a bank apartment fifteen feet by seventeen feet eight inches. The castle, on the holding of William Orr and William Christy, was flattened between 1824 and 1830.

The fourth important freehold was that of Manus McCowey Ballagh O'Cahan, lying south of the Aghadowey River in the Barony of Coleraine. His ancestors dated back to the fifteenth century and their home was Bovagh Castle. Tristram Beresford of Coleraine made a will, dated 23 October 1647, leaving the townlands purchased of Manus McCowey Ballagh O'Cahan with its ironworks to his grandson Randall Beresford. At the time of the Ordnance Survey it is recorded that Bovagh Castle was sold to Tristram Beresford for a horse, a fine suit of English clothes and a small sum of money. The O'Cahan who sold his lands was quite eccentric, and in the middle of the eighteenth century the castle was reported to have been let to a Donald Oge O'Cahan, who was the descendant of the original settlers. He had a son, John, who, like his father, was an attorney. They made a rough road through the castle grounds, built by his poorer tenants as part payment for their fees. In 1798 Bovagh Castle was used as a military post to control the surrounding countryside. A lament was written for Manus O'Cahan:

> Oh, princely Manus, man of noble soul
> Kinsman of bishops and of prisoners too
> It gives me heart to see these men low
> Beneath the cold flag as a bed of earth!
> . . . And let me not forget it castle Roe.

A few of the women of Aghadowey Parish appear to have been in very poor circumstances. On the poor list of 1702 appears the name of Grany and Noaly O'Cahan, and this appertained for a number of years.

The fifth important freehold was in the Ballymullan district running to Sewell Mountain. It belonged to Tomlyn and Owen Keogh O'Mullan. They were succeeded by Owen McShane O'Mullan. About 1619 Owen McShane sold five townlands in what was later Learmount Parish to Thomas Skipton. There were quite a number of townlands, and at the time of the Civil Survey they were held by the heir of Edmund Warren. The will of Owen Murray O'Mullan, of Ballymullan, was admitted to probate in 1638. He retained a number of townlands which passed to his son and heir, Tomlyn O'Mullan, who was described as an Irish Protestant. These townlands remained in the O'Mullan family for about a century or more. They turn up again in a deed dated 13 November 1707. Tomlyn favoured his eldest son, Patrick, and left him land in the area of Altimore, subject to Patrick paying a debt of £50 made by his father, and due to Ralph Green who resided in the parish of Glendermott. Half of the land in which Tomlyn lived was to pass to his son, George, and the other half to John. George and John were to repay to Thomas O'Mullan a debt not exceeding £20 due by their father to Robert Dilland and his wife at the Waterside in Londonderry.

Tomlyn was concerned that the property should not be alienated. He inserted a clause in the deed to the effect that George and John should not sell or mortgage the property without consent in writing of Patrick Mullan or his heirs. They could not let the property for more than a period of twenty-one years. Towards the middle of the century there emerged a series of deeds appertaining to these three townlands. In 1740 Thomas Mullan of Altimore received a gift of £100 from William Smith of Lisdillan, County Londonderry, for ever. The townland of Tamnagh, which was in the possession of Thomas Mullan, son of Connolly

McCauseland of Fruithill was let for ever. The townland of Tamnagh was in the possession of his undertakers. In 1747 Thomas O'Mullan sold to Connolly McCauseland of Fruit Hill for ever the townland of Dreen. However, the land was encumbered with an annuity; as in 1751 there was a deed arising between Mary Mullan, widow of James Mullan of Altimore. There was also a deed between Connolly McCauseland and Thomas Smyth of Newtownabbey. It mentioned articles drawn up by Patrick Mullan and Thomas Mullan. Patrick agreed to pay Mary Mullan £100 after the death of Thomas. It mentioned that Thomas Mullan in his lifetime should bestow the lands of Dreen, Tamnagh and Altimore to trustees in 1745 to pay Mary Mullan £30 per annum for life. It also mentioned that in 1714 there were some judgements obtained against Thomas Mullan in the Exchequer Court for a £400 debt to Mary Mullan. By the deed of 1751 Mary Mullan signed over land to Connolly McCauseland and Thomas Smyth for £250 in a court judgement. There was also an annuity and the sum of £100 with interest.

There were other difficulties in the way of the transfer. There are further deeds of 1750 and 1757 in which men and women are mentioned. The final transfer is to Connolly McCauseland of Fruithill and Thomas Smith of Limavady. This was perhaps the last County Londonderry freehold erected at the plantation to remain in existence, and it disappeared finally in 1517. Some of the smaller freeholders disappeared during the rebellion of 1641. The freehold in the parish of Cumber was forfeited by Gilleglass McCorry O'Cahan; and the freehold of Knockan, in the parish of Banagher let to Rory McShane O'Cahan was also forfeited. The freehold of Gilduff Oge Mullan in the parish of Dungiven was forfeited by his son. Shane was a Roman Catholic, differing from two others who were Protestants. The Gilduff Oge family played an active role in the 1641 Rebellion.

Manus McGilreagh O'Mullan held the third freehold in Cloughan. He remained on friendly terms with the retinue of Sir Thomas Phillips, as shown by an incident in January 1615 when Donnell McManus brought home his bride. A census in 1659 showed two Irish persons residing in Cloughan. A roll of 1665 records four families in the townland: Donnell McManus O'Mullan, Donnoghy O'Mullan, Neal O'Mullan and Brian O'Mullan.

In 1681 there was a Chancery action between Donoughy McDonnell McManus and Kilner Brazier. As Kilner was a minor, the action took place against his guardians. Donoughy claimed that his father had armed the townland of Cloughan and had paid Paul Brazier £100 in 1663. The mortgage was redeemable on 1 November 1616. Donnell McManus had died shortly before this. After his death and after the redemption had expired, his son applied to Brazier to redeem it. Donoughy O'Mullan said that the matter had been referred to the arbitration of George Phillips. He made the award in writing that Donoughy O'Mullan should continue in occupation paying rent of £20 per year, which would be paid regularly until the principal and interest were paid off. This was regularly paid until Paul Brazier's death. In 1675 Davenport captured six cows, two heifers and fourteen sheep from the landlords. He took O'Mullan prisoner, holding him at Davenport's house for three days and four nights.

The defendant's answer was to deny Phillip's award. Donoughy O'Mullan had sold his right of redemption of the mortgage paid to Paul Brazier. By deed of 6 November he let the land to O'Mullan for twenty-one years at £20 per annum. Davenport admitted that he had carried off cattle in payment for £20 rent due since Brazier's death. He also admitted that he got the plaintiff arrested by the sherrif's officer. Davenport however for some reason released him on the promise to pay up. Davenport claimed that Donnoghy O'Mullan was unable to hold the land and pay rent. In 1678 or 1680 he surrendered the leases, upon which the land was rented to Robery Huey. This was not the end of the matter. In 1727 John O'Mullan of Dublin brought an action against Kilner Brazier, son of Paul Brazier, to whom his great-grandfather had mortgaged Cloughar. The plan was to redeem the mortgage. Joining the defendants were William Ross, assignee of Brazier's interest, and a long number of others, including Robert White, John Hopkins, William Anderson and David Linton. Some were named as tenants of the townland. The lands that had been occupied by the Irish in 1659 were now completely tenanted by colonizers.

The next freehold to be dealt with was that of the McGilligans. This sept had originally come from the Bradagh district of Inishowen some centuries before the plantation and had settled in the lands beneath Benevenagh just opposite their original home across Lough Foyle. Here the land belonged to the Church and the McGilligans were hereditary tenants. They gave their name to the region – Magilligan. At the time of the plantation, Brian Bane McGilligan was granted freehold land at Ballycartan in the Aghanloe parish. Manus O'Cahan and Gilduffe McBrian O'Cahan were fined for living in a house instead of building an English-style home. The family took part in the 1641 Rebellion and the freehold was confiscated from Manus McGilligan, who was made a freeman of Limavady.

Ballycarton was leased by Sir Marcus Beresford to Captain William Lane, who was the agent in Ireland of the Hon The Irish Society. Lane was an ancestor of the Lanes of Rush Hall. Another well-known family was the Boyles. James Boyle came from Scotland and settled in the region about 1660. The family house had been at Spring Hill. From here they moved to Bridge Hill House, built in 1732. The other important confiscation took place following the 1641 Rebellion, affecting the O'Cahan clan. McHenry O'Cahan of the Loughan and the O'Cahans of Dunseverick had land confiscated. In January 1647 a warrant was issued for Captain Tristram Beresford to occupy the lands of James Oge McHenry of the Loughan. In 1653 they were put in charge of the lands by the Church, and paid a rent of £90 per annum until the sum of £800 was paid. The Church had a long connection with Coleraine. Here there was a flour mill near the town and also a paper mill at the Tulland. The paper mill had been built in 1749. It processed rags into pulp from which brown paper was manufactured.

The McHenry O'Cahans, during the time of the plantation, were known as McHenry, but occasionally O'Cahan is added. We find here that McHenry was being used as a surname, arising from the original Henry O'Cahan. The McHenrys owned a great deal of land in the parishes of Ballyrashane and Ballywilliam.

After the 1641 Rebellion, Gillduffe O'Cahan of Dunseverick was examined in March 1654 about the part he played with his sons and sons-in-law in the 1641 Rebellion. O'Cahan had married a daughter of Cahill O'Hara of Loughguile, by whom he had three sons and two daughters who married Henry McHenry O'Cahan and Brian Modder McHenry O'Cahan. Gilduffe senior had some very bleak views about the position at Dunseverick in the Route of North Antrim during the rebellion. He began to hear Mass at Dunluce, where he had something to drink with his son, Manus, and Henry McHenry, his son-in-law. Between one and two in the afternoon Captain McPhedris and a dozen horsemen had arrived at Dunluce Castle. As mentioned, Captain Digby had not yielded to pressure from McPhedris and his party to surrender the castle.

Ballintoy Church was plundered, but three of his assailants were killed by shots from the clergy; and he himself – Gillduffe – was hit upon the headpiece by a stone and thrown to the ground. His son Turlough Oge and some others once again attacked the church. They tried to break down the walls with pickaxes but were ejected. Gillduffe and his son, Turlough Oge, were executed for their part in the rebellion. Dunseverick Castle and surrounding lands were possessed a few years afterwards and Dunluce Castle fell into ruin. The remaining history of Dunluce and the O'Cahans is of great interest.

The Annals record that O'Cahan, chief of the Cianachta, was killed by Manus Manus O'Cahan, whose territory he had invested as far as Armoy. This entry in the Annals records an O'Cahan resident at Dunluce in the territory of North Antrim. Between 1524 and 1526 there was a succession of feuds amongst the O'Cahans. It is mentioned in the Annals under 1525 that John, a candidate for the chieftancy, was killed by a party of his own men, including the son of Rory of the Route. Rory of the Route can be identified with the Rory who was a brother of Donough the Hospitable and Donnell the Cleric. There was the genealogy of the chiefs for Aibhne, who was drowned in 1577, whose grandson was Rory of the Route. The O'Cahans were later seen at Dunseverick. It is difficult to imagine for legal reasons why they put up a candidate as chief of the O'Cahans of Londonderry.

The strength of the O'Cahans of Dunseverick on the eve of the rebellion is seen by the list of pardons granted to Randal McDonnell and his inferiors. There are a number of names, including Bernard, Rorie Oge, Shaeine and Gillpatrick.

The O'Cahans of Dunseverick played a role in the 1641 Rebellion, and one of them was executed along with his son. The castle was confiscated a few years later, after which it fell into ruin. Robert McCahan in his description of Dunseverick Castle claims the remnants of the O'Cahans continued to live in the area about six miles from the castle, which was called Ballinlea O'Cahan. Twelve of the O'Cahans were living in the district according to the Annals. Charles O'Cahan mortgaged Ballinla in 1748, but the name O'Cahan eventually disappeared in the Barony of Carey, which covered the district.

McCaughan or McCahan are names that occur in North-East Ulster, but they are rare elsewhere. The tradition is that their names should be O'Cahan and not simply names of their clans. In adopting English surnames some of the O'Cahans of the Route changed their names to McCaughan or McCahon, whilst others changed their names to McKane or Kane. The change of name has an excellent example in the case of Richard Kane, Governor of Minora. There is little concrete evidence of a change from O'Cahan to McCaughan.

The name McCaughan has many spellings. Robert McCahan in his pamphlet lists ten families. McCaughan is sometimes changed to Caughey or McCaughey. An indenture of 25 September 1773 mentions Robert Kaghey, sometimes known as Robert McCahan of Belfast. Apart from the 'Mc' or 'O', the Route name can be spelled the same way as the Derry name 'O'Cahan'. Bryan Roe O'Caghan of Errigal Parish appears in the Chancery Bill of 1687, already mentioned. More names are recorded in the Limavady records of 1664. 'Mc' and 'O' both mean 'son of'. The jury list of Sir Donnell O'Cahan appears to use McKonor and O'Konor as being interchangeable along with other names.

The McCaughans of North Antrim were prominent in farming and business. They derive from Patrick McCaughan, who was born in 1746 and died in 1830. He had married Rose Stuart and, through him, many of the McCaughans of today derive their name. In the Northern Ireland Public Records Office, the family-tree records the McCaughans, who were Presbyterians. One went on to be founder of O'Cahan's sugar refinery in the United States. Other O'Cahans in North Antrim became O'Kanes. O'Laverty records that, until about sixty years before the event, the O'Kanes would come to the old castle at Ballylough. They had plenty of food and dined beside its ruined walls. They now laid claim to their ancient family possessions.

The other O'Mullans can be mentioned. Thomas O'Mullan, a gentleman of Faughanvale, was one of the sureties of Henry O'Crilly, a parish priest and two other parishes under the 1704 Act for registration of parish priests. He was also a surety for Roger McClosky, Pastor of Dungiven and Faughanvale. The next O'Mullan was Shane Roe O'Mullan, also a gentleman. He is described as late of Somerset, County Londonderry and also late of Culnasilag. The family appear in the Chancery Bill of 30 April 1687. The plaintiffs were Shane Roe's younger children. The defendants were Shane O'Mullan, minor son of Manus O'Mullan, of Somerset, deceased. He was the eldest son of Shane Roe. The plaintiffs said that Shane Roe O'Mullan had bought the townland of Altduff from John Brown and got a new deed made out for himself and his wife, Margaret, and their issue. Manus had been entrusted with the deed for the townland. Manus had obtained the deed in 1684 and had died in 1685, leaving in his will minor son, Shane. Frederick Hamilton had been appointed guardian. They requested that the new deed be set aside, and that Mary Brown should be entrusted to make another deed according to their father's will.

There is no answer, but it is recorded that the prerogative court on 26 June 1682 granted the administration of the estate to Shane Roe O'Mullan of County Londonderry (a gentleman, but deceased), to his son Manus O'Mullan. Shane Roe is said to have died without a will. In July 1709, John Mullen, of the city of Dublin (also a gentleman) transferred the 250 acres of Altduff to the Honourable Major General Frederick Hamilton and his heirs for ever, if £120 were paid to him.

Somerset was originally the seat of the George family, the first of whom was a Cromwellian soldier. They built a brick castle which commanded a lovely view of the river Bann. The outside walls were painted red and the castle was known to travellers as the Red Castle. Upon Squire George's death, the building was neglected and fell into ruin. At the time of the Ordnance Survey only a remnant of the kitchen remained, the rest of the castle having been pulled down. The Georges did not occupy the property for long, for Somerset was bought by Mr

William Richardson in 1726. Richardson eventually acquired a large estate in the parish of Macosquin. Somerset House is said to have been built by the Richardsons in 1732 and enlarged in 1822. In the statistical survey of the county of Londonderry in 1802 it was said that the Richardsons were keen planters and improvers in the county. This was perhaps Henry Richardson, formerly of Bengal, who died at Somerset in 1786. The estate was sold to the tenants at the close of the nineteenth century.

The freeholders were disappearing and a new manor house stood and took its place in the rush for land. It is interesting who were the first colonizers in the Derry area. Confiscation of course had been made following the rebellion. The freeholders do not seem to hold onto their lands. The O'Cahans and their close followers and many others belonged to a society in which the clan leaders were noted for their military prowess. At the time of the colonization, they were pushed into a more complex community where pursuing business was more important than honourable warfare. The legal quarrels in which they had become involved could not be cut with impunity by a revenging or ordinary sword. For conditions in Ulster they were unprepared and they were unable to adapt quickly enough to the changes in circumstances. The O'Cahans, as a ruling landlord class, disappeared completely from the county in which they ruled for five centuries. Some of them, however, found themselves more at home in the French and Spanish Armies. Some fell into the lower ranks of the community. It was the ordinary followers of the clans who had had to struggle for existence, and who survived as farmers on the land of their fathers and labourers on the land. Some of the new landlords can be mentioned here: the Phillips family were well known in the Limavady district during the centuries following the seventeenth-century colonization. Sir Thomas Phillips had a notable dispute with the founder companies in the earlier years of the century, and his sons Dudley and Thomas took a leading role in the 1641 Rebellion. George Phillips, son of Dudley, was the major figure in the Limavady plantation from the time of the settlement until he died as a very old man near the end of the century. The Phillips' estate was bought by the Reverend William Connolly of Castletown, County Kildare in the south of Ireland and Speaker of the Commons. Connolly lived at Roe Park as well as at Daisy Hill, Limavady, and died in 1729. The wearing of women's scarves at funerals was a widespread practice, and this encouraged the linen industry. By his will, Robert McCauseland of Fruit Hill, succeeded to the estates in County Londonderry (Derry). The McCauselands were of Scots origins, where the name is often written as McAuslane. This family had kept an unbroken connection with Limavady since their colonizing years. The present representative of the family is Colonel Connolly McCauseland.

The Right Honourable William Connolly, who died without having children, left other property to his nephew, and also to the Right Honourable Thomas Connolly. He issued the following warning in 1788: he expected that all of his tenants should be bound by their leases to the Manor Hill of Newtown, and that they should grind their own corn, which grew on the estate of the mill only. They would enjoy Connolly's favour. Rent had to be paid on five of his lands. Some places needed supplies of water, and he authorized Mr Ross, his landlord agent, to make the tenants pay rent regularly.

The OS Memoirs of around 1835 stated that the town of Limavady was almost a modern creation, as far as houses were concerned. They pointed out that half a century before it consisted of a few cabins and houses in Main Street. The O'Connollys wanted to rebuild it in the form of a diamond, but this idea was abandoned. Limavady was left to expand according to its circumstances. By the close of the eighteenth century, Sampson favoured those who had improved their property. Amongst those he mentioned were such names as Mr McCauseland of Fruit Hill, Mr Dominick McCauseland of Daisy Hill and the Reverend Hamilton of Bessbrook. Mr Ross of the Lodge had a smart dwelling situated on the banks of the river Roe, close to Newtown; here there were a lot of trees. A Mr Campbell had a large garden with sturdy brick walls.

In the two centuries following the plantation many names were made in business. Business was not despised by the early planters. They had a great interest in fishing, fairs, mills and distilling. Sir Robert Phillips obtained a licence to manufacture whiskey in County Coleraine. The Reverend Andrew Alexander, a Presbyterian minister, had a son, Andrew of Ballychose, Newtown Limavady. He first of all married Jessie, daughter of Sir Thomas Phillips, by whom he had a son and heir, Jacob Alexander. His second marriage was to the daughter of the Laird of Hilles, by whom he had a son, who was ancestor of the Earls of Caledon.

Jacob Alexander remained in Ulster and married Margaret Oliver, daughter and heiress of John Oliver of the Lodge, Newtown Limavady. The family made a name for themselves as businessmen and merchants. In 1782 there are three names mentioned as bleachers in the Limavady area. From Jacob Alexander was descended Maxwell Alexander, of Roe Park, whose sisters were also married. At the time of Pynnar's survey, Dungiven Castle and bawn were in the possession of Lady Doddington, whose husband had built the castle. She was the daughter of Tristram Beresford and afterwards became Lady Cooke upon her marriage to Sir Francis Cooke. Lady Doddington held her estate from the Skinners company. At the close of the seventeenth century the estate fell to Edward

Carey, who lived in the old castle and planters' bawn. Henry Carey, in 1742, obtained a fresh lease on the old castle at a rental of £600,000, as the payment of a lump sum of £5,637 to the Skinners.

Another family came from Scotland; John Ogilby, MD from Aberdeen settled in Limavady. There were also registered bleachers. Robert Ogilby was a Dublin linen merchant and he gave the Right Honourable Henry Carey £10,000 for the remainder of his lease, which expired in 1803. He obtained a new lease from the Skinners at £25,000. By 1838 there was only one storey of the old castle remaining. The following year the Ogilbys spent a large sum of money rebuilding the castle. However, it remained unfinished and the Ogilbys took up residence at Pelliper House. The bawn, or castle enclosure at Dungiven is the original bawn built during the plantation.

Some of the original farmers of the London companies' estates retained a long relationship with the district. George Canning, agent of the Ironmongers, came from Warwickshire, and his family had a long connection with the Garavagh district. A descendant was created Lord Garvagh, but other families were out of luck. Sir Robert McClelland farmed his proportion of the Haberdashers' and Clothworkers' estates, his headquarters being at Ballycastle. Pynnar said that the castle was well finished being very strong 'and well wrought'. Sir Robert and his wife dwelled therein. His daughter and next heir, Maria, was married to a Scotsman. Sir Robert Maxwell succeeded his father at Ballycastle. Eventually the Haberdashers sold their estates to the Beresford family, who had many lands in County Londonderry. Tristram Beresford, son of a Kentish squire, settled at Coleraine during the plantation. He was full of energy and had been appointed as a subordinate agent of the London companies. He died in 1647. He had amassed a lot of property at Coleraine and further afield, and he left the abbey house in which Captain McLellan was living to his daughter. Also walled were the two fields called Mount Sandy Fields abutting the highway on the road to Coleraine. Also there were six and a half townlands in the parish of Dunboe with eleven townlands called rangelands in the same parish. These townlands were leased from the Bishop of Derry. Also walled was all the corn and grain stacked at the bawn in the parish of Coleraine. Now there were ten townlands belonging to Captain Manus O'Cahan; some were bought from Manus McCowy Ballagh O'Cahan with its ironworks; his present dwelling house with its out-offices, brewing-house yard, milk house, dairy house, gardens and orchard came under review. He also willed all the other houses, lands and tenements within the town and parish of Coleraine.

His two sons looked after the great fortune that their father had left them. Michael, the youngest, was a commissioner in the Civil Survey and Revenue. Tristram, the eldest, was made a baronet. Sir Tristram's grandson was created Earl of Tyrone. Later on the family was represented by the Marquis of Waterford. In Coleraine the family name was venerated in the place named Beresford Place. In 1716 Sir Marcus Beresford of County Meath created Richard Fenner of Dublin tenant of the freehold of the manor of Freemore to the manor of the Haberdashers. The manor had four castles, 600 cottages, six mills, 1,000 gardens, sixty orchards, 2,000 acres of pasture, 200 acres of wood, 300 acres of moor and a hundred acres of marsh.

The eighteenth century in County Londonderry, as far as property and possessions were concerned, saw the end of the old aristocracy who were chiefs of the clans. A new landlord gentry took their place, versed in business, law and the power of money. The clan system lingered on in song and story. At the meeting of the harpers in Belfast in 1792 one of them playing the old tunes was Denis O'Hempsey, the blind harper of Magilligan. He is said to have lived until he was 112. He had been blinded as the result of smallpox at the age of three. He was taught the harp by Bridget O'Cahan. It was not only the O'Cahan ways that were tolerated. The blind Rory Dall O'Cahan is remembered as one of the chiefs. He was also a celebrated harper. At the harpers meeting of 1792, the names of the estates to which he was entitled were still being processed. The glories of the past, however, only lingered on in song and story.

101

# Chapter 12

## *Back to Square One*

After the 1641 Rebellion there are only a few references to the clans and it is hard to slot them into place in history. Few had property to make wills and execute conveyances. Those who rebelled against society, however, are mentioned. As far as Church and state are concerned quiet law-abiding folk are mentioned in the records. In the sixteenth century there is a letter from Cahal Daniel O'Cahan to Owen O'Rourke, suggesting a combined effort at managing their estates. O'Cahan is pictured as a person of no estate or fortune in the kingdom, though a bold and daring man. Orders were sent out from the Sheriffs of Donegal and Londonderry to arrest him. Donegal was where he generally lived. In 1688 there was a proclamation from the Lord Deputy and Council listing a series of people guilty of appearing in arms against the King's will. Some had committed murders, robberies and other offences, and had escaped into the woods and mountains. Listed are Bryan Roe, Shane O'Cahan, Patrick McCormick O'Hagan, Patrick and Shane O'Hagan and Edmund O'Moylan. The first two were the former residents in the Barony of Dungannon; the last were residents in the parish of Ballinascreen. In 1677 the Lord Mayor of Coleraine was informed against a certain Art O'Mullan. This was opposed by the Mayor of Coleraine Corporation, who said that the information was false. In 1735 an abduction was the centre of a legal inquiry, when Roger O'Cahan of Kilrea with others carried off Sarah Thompson of Drumcroon, with a view to marriage.

The most notorious figure was the outlaw Shane Crossagh O'Mullan. Beyond Dungiven, in the mountains, stories are told of his adventures as if they had only happened a while ago. He was the Derry Robin Hood and he has inspired many poets in a way that not even the O'Cahans had dreamed. However, information is very scanty about the period.

Change came to Ulster in 1714, and the situation was very difficult. There are many years of drought recorded and there were bad harvests in 1725, 1726 and 1727. In 1728 the price of food stood at a long-time high. It was out of these troubles that Shane Crossagh emerged. He originally lived at Frenagh, lying east of Donald's Hill. He is said to have been ejected by the Richardson family. He first came to attention in 1729 when his large home at Vow was burned. A Cromwellian officer, Captain John Galland was given lands in the area, afterwards known as Finvoy Estate, and he lived at Vow. This house was to be the scene of Shane Crossagh's activities. James Kerr of Finvoy was examined in 1729. He claimed that he was assaulted and knocked down on the main road at Vow by Robert Harrison; 6/9d was taken out of his pocket by him. On the 17th he was on the road to Rasharkin. The group consisted of Richard Galland of Vow, Michael Mullan, James Murphy and Mattehew McCaly, all of Vow. Kerr was ushered into the inn of John Miller in Rasharkin at about eight o'clock in the morning. His captors, he claimed, had beaten and kicked him and tied his hands with cord. He said that Shane O'Mullan had flashed a broadsword at him many times, which frightened Kerr, who pleaded for his life. Another contender carried water. They forced Kerr to drink two quarts of it at a time. Shane O'Mullan removed the silk handkerchief from around his neck. Kerr said that he had been held at the inn until six o'clock in the evening, after which he was taken to Vow.

The group now charged with their guns and swords were drawn. They went to the house of Joseph Moore of Rasharkin. They swore that as soon as Moore's house was open they would get him to eat and then drive him into Hell. Kerr, however, concludes that Moore's doors were shut.

Some three weeks afterwards James Carr of Lisseghan in Finvoy Parish gave evidence about the attack on their mansion house of Vow. Here had resided William Galland of Vow, deceased, but James Carr was now in possession of William Moore's lands, whose servants were resident on it. There were valuable goods in the mansion, including beds and hangings, tables and chairs, meal, butter and cheese. But on 7 June, a Sunday, Carr observed a large number of men with guns and bayonets marching in great agitation towards Vow. They had fired several shots at it, and called to Moore's servants to get out of the house or they would burn it down. Robert Glas of Rasharkin took up the story. He said that William Gay and his servants and smiths had made some iron slugs into bullets. The slugs were carried by Harrison in a pot; his associates fired a second volley. The house was engulfed in flames. Moore's servants had to flee from it, and it was reduced to ashes. Eleven witnesses observed the arson attack, amongst them being Richard Gallard of Vow, Robert Taylor and Owen Roe O'Neill.

There is a lot more to the story than is made out. Richard Gallard of

Vow and Kennedy Stafford, both gentlemen, were concerned with the burning. At the assizes, held at Carrickfergus on 23 July 1729, a number of notables were concerned with the matter and were said to be out in arms and holding His Majesty's position in Ulster. The two O'Mullans were also concerned with the affair, and one is described as a yeoman. Richard Gallard of Vow was not outlawed until July 1730, the following year.

Shane Crossagh now led an exciting life as an outlaw, mainly amongst the moors and mountains of Londonderry. There is a particular site connected with him – the stones on Crossagh's mountain. Shane Crossagh was captured by soldiers. The escort rested at Carntogher Mountain (in ancient times there was no road which crossed Carntogher to Dungiven). Shane challenged the soldiers to a leaping match. When Shane's turn came he made three great leaps and on the last leap he bounded down the mountainside in order to escape.

The Ordnance Survey officers were informed of another tradition about the origin of these stones. They were told that on certain occasions the youth of many of the parishes from the Baronies of Keenaught, Tirkeeran and Loughinsolin gathered together at Carntogher for casting shoulder stones, jumping and other parties. Keenaught had been successful for many years, but on one occasion Loughinsolin seemed to be getting the better of it. James McGilligan of Cashel in the south of Ireland and a farmer, was about forty years of age. Upon hearing about the difficulties of his barony, he looked at the amazing jumps made by the Loughinsolin men. He ordered a pint of poteen. He had a good drink and made three such leaps that had never been equalled in Carntogher before or since. Some time later Shane Crossagh was in the area. He was in the habit of having plenty to drink and giving money to those who sheltered him. He let some of the country folk have drinks in order to circulate the tale that it was he that made the great leaps at Carntogher. This robbery was well known and the reports gained credence, and the leaps were attributed to Shane Crossagh. This was reported to the survey officers by Owen McCloskey, the storyteller or sennachie and many others. His informants claimed that Shane Crossagh robbed the rich and poor alike, in contrast to a Robin Hood reputation of robbing the rich alone and helping the poor.

Another place associated with this outlaw, Shane Crossagh, is the General's Bridge, near Feeny. It is said that he held up a general and a party of soldiers by laying caps on the turf alongside a ditch, in order to give the impression that they were armed men in ambush. The strategy was successful and Shane disarmed the general and his men. There is a third place connected with him – a hidden place, where the Bavn-Tollaght joins the river Faughan. Eventually Shane and his assailants were captured and hanged. More legends blossomed around his name. The officers of the survey were told a tradition about his children. The man was Shane O'Mullin descended on his mother's side from the O'Cahans. When looking at his stock one morning he heard a child cry and found it on the ground covered in cloth. He took the baby home. He and his wife reared him and left him a large portion of their property. According to the story this baby was the great-grandfather of Shane Crossagh. Shane's grandfather settled at Clogan in Banagher Parish. Eventually Shane Crossagh, his father and others were hanged.

Legend blossomed around the birth. When he knew that he was going to be hanged at Dungiven, he asked if there were any Dungiven men there. Those who told the tale were sure that if there had been any credence to it, lots of people would know. They would have found out the place where gold was hidden. The Ordnance Survey folk were informed of the very large stones in the townland of Creggan in Banagher, not troubled until 1784. Now Manus O'Mullan said that there was a large stone of ritualistic significance, and that there was gold under it. He travelled to the spot and met a female dressed in green who told him where to dig. He at last found the treasure. Members of his family prospered, along with his cattle. This was Shane Crossagh's gold, found in the same townland. Some say that a foalskin of gold lay buried in a fairy thorn, a short distance from the spot near Tit-Kane – it was Shane Crossagh's gold.

Agrarian unrest continued throughout the eighteenth century, breaking out into violence at times when houses, turf, hay or corn were burned. The cattle were killed or maimed. At Limavady a group of tenants seemed to be content with their lot. One Saturday afternoon about one o'clock, the Right Honourable Thomas Connolly passed through Dungiven, where he was saluted by the Dungiven corps of volunteers, drawn up there to greet him. About two miles from Dungiven a numerous body of his Limavady freehold tenants, numbering about 200, met with lifted hearts at seeing their landlord. These, together with other corps, escorted him to Newtown, where Lord de la Poer's regiment, consisting of a general, a colonel, two lieutenant colonels and nearly 200 men were drawn up to salute him. He now proceeded with an escort to Fruit Hill, the headquarters of Connolly McCauseland, Esq. Here the battalion fired three volleys, and returned to the town.

In the Bovevagh Parish the officers of the survey were informed that the most remarkable event in the parish took place in recent times, which was the murder of Brian Backagh McCloskey in the year 1793. He was supposed to be giving evidence on behalf of the Skinners to the Reverend

John Harvey, whose soldiers had been wiped out. McCloskey's home was set on fire by a party at midnight. He tried to escape through a window, but was unsuccessful. His mother and sister, now surrounded, stood under the door jambs. They were protected by thick walls. The draught through the chinks of the door carried the flames away from them. However, they were rescued by others who had appeared upon the scene before their position became too dangerous. McCloskey's mother was dead, so it was announced to the officers. The daughter was not present in the parish.

The Reverend John Harvey was the minister concerned and he was installed in Bovevagh on 17 April 1794. The Skinners appear in a diary – that of John Macky, who died in 1809. He was engaged by Lady Hamilton in 1786 as a clerk at Cranagh fishery. In the following year he was appointed inspector of rivers. He rode and walked through the area for fourteen years. He recorded vivid pictures of life at the time, together with comments on his daily work. The Skinners at Dunboe (who assembled every night at the river Bann) were poaching the salmon. Macky accompanied the Mayor of Coleraine to Colonel Warbuton and applied for assistance against them. He got no encouragement and Macky commented that he saw fresh salmon in the kitchen being cooked. He was described as 'this old lowlid Taitor'.

He was employed as water-keeper for the various rivers. Several of these employed were Mullans and Mallons. There was water-keeping in 1791 at the Bovevagh River; in 1795 at the Garvach River; and again in 1797. There was increasing unrest in 1798 as rebellion approached. Macky was sent threatening letters dated from Dunboe, and they were left at his door at night. Once he spent the night at Sandy Hills, and he saw two fishing boats; by daylight they had caught fish and taken them for sale in the countryside. There were three men with guns guarding them. As he progressed he met with crowds of Defenders, one of the groups that rose during these troubled years. By October 1796 Macky noted that no one would elect to be keeper at Mettigan and Glenullar Rivers. Those involved claimed that they were threatened, but they would not say by whom. In 1797 the same position obtained. Macky said that at Mettigan there were various villains. He noted that the rivers carried a lot of waste for the season. J. McAllen warned him not to go out on the river, but said that he would try to obtain all the nets and bring them to Macky.

By 1795 one of the keepers was distinguished by the title 'Mac'. The family inhabited the region of the rivers for three years. In 1798 Macky noted in his diary that he went up to Glenullar, and not finding the keepers he spent the night with rheumatism in his body. In 1799 a member of the family retained in the person of George the name Mullan. By now the

1798 Rebellion was over. Macky was at his sister's, watching the workmen repairing their home. He records the conflicts that took place on Monday 28 July. The workers were on low wages, from 2/8d to 3/3d per day. He could never see more than two or three men working at any one time.

A generation passed before some insight is given into the clans by the Ordnance Survey. Dr O'Donovan passed a lot of time in the parish of Errigal. He met an old man who said that he was chief of the O'Mullans. O'Donovan composed a poem about him, for he was greatly taken by the sept of the O'Mullan (Brian Mor). He was in poor condition, but he may well have been liked by Lord Garvagh and his neighbours for his honesty and principles. In the Annals of the Four Masters he is described as a man of truth and honour, sumptuous, warlike and hospitable. Another poem said that the Gaels looked upon Brian as their chief. Brian had fine feelings and noble thoughts, sitting by the fire in his lonely cabin. As the senior member of his famous family, his heart rejoiced when he heard the name of O'Mullan, with the title of Manus.

Brian told Manus his life story. He was a member of the United Irishmen in 1798 and some of his followers had been hanged. Brian fled and led his own life in disguise. Lord Garvagh, his friend, knowing his honesty, had procured him a pardon and protection. Brian had run up debts to the tune of £1,800. To pay this off he sold his rich farms and beautiful home. Lord Garvagh bestowed upon Brian the mountain farm of Brockaghboy, and Brian went to live there, looking out into the mountains and wastelands. Brian was poor and looked upon himself as a conquered chief. His son left him and wrote from South America, saying that he was worth more money than his father ever possessed in Glenullar. He said that he was not in a position to redeem the farms as Brian would have wanted. Brian seemed not to care about the predicament. He had maintained his good name throughout all adversity and would die an honest man as Brian Manus Mullan. The meaning of the name Manus is not readily understood.

O'Donovan was interested in Brian Manus as a person and was also interested in the local lore, and his explanation of place names. Brian was interested in the ancient tales, as a poem goes to show. He talked of his country's ancient pride: Old Aleach in Donegal was in grandeur, seat of the Northern Kings. O'Donovan took down the work of Brian Manus, describing the march of the Clan Mullan. The poem goes:

> I will walk the great road,
> I will walk the great road,
> No thanks to my enemies.

He also recorded Gaelic lines on the subject of Keenaught, and the different names of Glenullen. According to one source the glen was originally called Gleanndushree in Irish, which meant the Black Glen of Red Hue. The soil was very mossy and boggy on the surface and grown over with heath of reddish colour. Now William MacFion was killed and buried in the glen, which was dedicated to him and called Glenullen.

'Mann' was used more than forty years previously in Macky's diary. It also appears after Brian Mann's time. In the Griffith Valuation of 1859 mention is made of the townland of Brockaghbog of Elizabeth Mann. The name Mann can be traced over a period of seventy years. Brian's other sayings are less easy of access. He says that the Feling an Dana had possessed thirty-two townlands in the area of Dunboe after the Ulster plantation. The OS Memoirs of Errigal Parish were taken in 1834 when Brian was over eighty. However, the O'Mullan chief was recognized in the closing years of the century by the O'Cahan and by the English. There is no mention of Feling in the pardons or in the jury list on any of the documents of the plantation of Ulster. These may have been extensive. O'Mullan's lands in Dunboe Parish were held at the same time as the plantation.

The O'Mullan pettigree was prepared to make a claim upon the McQuillan legacy. This is probably the legacy mentioned in the McQuillan manuscript history. A McQuillan who died at Versailles some time before left a large estate to the nearest heir of the name McQuillan and house of Dunluce. Edward McQuillan was born in 1760. He said that his father had travelled to France to claim the legacy. He also went to Jesus College at Versailles, which was the trustees of the property of all officers of the Irish Brigade in France. France was in turmoil about the expulsion of the Jesuits. He was arrested, and all his belongings were taken from him.

Brian Mann said that he was to be buried in Errigal graveyard, according to a poem Brian wrote about him. No tombstone bearing his name is extant for it was likely in the circumstances that there would be no tombstone. Mr James Mullan of Castlerock (deceased) said that he could trace his family to Brian Mann O'Mullan of Feling an Dana. The Castlerock family came from Terrydoo. The town of Terrydoo passed out of their possession, but the Mullans of Templemoyle and Artikelly are the same family. The Mullan family has always kept up close contact with the area. The area surrounds Keady, Body's Mountain, and Donald's Hill through Glen Mullen up to Courtcosoreagh and Benbradagh. There have been Mullans in other important places including Terrydoo, all of these being townlands.

In these areas there was a feeling of clan solidarity, but the clan feuds continued in modified form. The feuds generally started by sitting up during St John's Eve and at dances. There was much drinking to excess; since the people were divided into class, events generally ended in a clan fight. At the time of the Ordnance Survey the officers were informed that in Errigal Parish the O'Mullans and O'Hagans had fallen out forty years before. At the time of the survey the fighting had become less frequent – not more than two fights having taken place in the previous eight years. About six years before the survey a challenge took place between one of the O'Mullans and one of the O'Hagans. Several hundred of the two clans made ready to fight, but they were dispersed by the Roman Catholic clergymen. The O'Hagans had a number of enemies since the war was also opposed by the O'Kanes and the McNicholls. However, the quarrels were settled. The O'Connells and the O'Kanes had fallen out twenty years before the survey, but the rift had been closed and they became good friends.

In the parish of Dungiven the leading clans were the O'Kanes and the McClookoys. The McCloskeys were descended from Blosky O'Cahan or O'Kane, as mentioned in the Annals of the Four Masters under the year 1196. In the Latin records of the Armagh registery details about the clans are recorded. It quotes the following: AD 1430 Marritius McBlosgaigh canonicus Dervenis; AD 1430 Dermicius McBlosgaid canonicus Devensis.

At the time of the Ordnance Survey the McCloskeys made up about two thirds of the population in Dungiven Parish. The O'Kanes and McCloskeys met at fairs and markets. A lot of drink flowed. Arguments settled around the relative positions of the two clans. They boasted that their ancestors had ruled the greater part of the county. The McCloskeys came from a long pettigree family and had superior numbers and much valour on the field of battle. In the district there was one regiment of 1,000 men, nicknamed the Yellow Stockings, and they were almost all McCloskeys. These clansmen were not only politicians, but were ready to take up pistol and sword. In 1830 there was a long dispute between O'Kane and McCloskey over a piece of land in the Benady Glen. The dispute was finally settled by the sword, bringing honour and credit to both sides. The place for the duel had been chosen, and on the day hundreds had flocked to watch. The two combatants arrived upon the scene with ancient family swords, but the police had got wind of the duel and arrived at the spot in time to put O'Kane and McCloskey under arrest.

The Rector of Banagher and Dungiven, the Reverend Alexander Ross, wrote to Reeves in 1850, providing him with information. He reported that one side of the Benady Glen was inhabited by the McCloskeys. The glen lay to the south-east of the river Roe. The most backward members of the clan were to be found in the townland of Cluntgeeragh, where Gaelic was still used. The Ossianic poems were handed down by tradition. Mr Ross claimed that there were two distinct families of McCloskeys in that area, one having red hair the other a fair complexion. They both had peculiarities. Other sources include the Annals of the Four Masters. O'Kelly in his gleanings of the history of Ulster mentions the townland of Dubhroa as the black spot on the river Roe. Brian Manus O'Mullin gave the former name of Glenullen as Glenannudushroe – the Black Glen of Red Hue.

The number of McCloskeys in Dungiven Parish was so large that each family at the time of the Ordnance Survey had to be distinguished by some sort of name, such as the colour of their hair, or size of body. The nicknames were in Gaelic, and were coupled with English names or surnames. It was impossible for a stranger coming into the area to locate McCloskey unless he knew the byname or nickname of the family concerned. Nicknames were used in letters, and some of these letters came from the United States of America – for example, Patrick 'Hamish' McCloskey and James 'Irvine' McCloskey. There was a similar system at work amongst the O'Mullans. An Ironmongers' list of tenants distinguishes two Patrick O'Mullans as Long Patrick and Short Patrick. Nicknames are still used by the O'Mullans of today.

The point which is stressed is that a clan homeland existed for use in plantation – and still exists today. The McCloskey headquarters were the Benady Glen, whose praises have been sung in poetry, and which have been translated by the survey officers. It ends by saying that it was not possible to find a glen like the glen of Benady. The foothills of the mountains running from Benevenagh to Carntogher was the homeland of the O'Cahans. The original settlement of the Owen clan lies just across Lough Foyle in Inishowen. From Glen Shane and Carntogher there is an interesting view towards Lough Neagh. The view takes in the lands conquered by the Owen clan in mid-Ulster – Tir-Owen means the land of Owen. From there many Ulstermen have emigrated to the United States, Australia and Africa – from Dunboy and Terrydoo and other obscure names. The emigrants have contributed a lot to the buildings of other lands. It is safe to say that they never forgot their origins. In 1965 the Roman Catholic church of Dungiven was renovated costing £25,000, the gift of a generous American millionaire, Mr Matthew McCloskey, who was formerly Ambassador to Ireland.

I would like to end this chapter by examining the role of the MacMillan clan. It has been mentioned that the Scots of Antrim crossed the North Channel to settle in Scotland in the fifth century from Antrim Dalriada to Argyll. They eventually gave their name to the whole of Scotland. The

Irish of Antrim were known as Scots. The name MacMillan in Scotland and the name O'Mullan in Ulster have a similar Gaelic origin. Mullan or Mullin means the Tonsured One, and the prefix 'O' and 'Mac' both mean 'Son of'. Both names mean 'Son of the Tonsured One'. This original connection is the only one that can be relied upon with confidence, but other connections are possible. Two of these connections can be mentioned.

Buchanan of Auchmar said that an O'Cahan came to Ireland to the Crown lands of Buchanan at the start of the eleventh century. The Buchanan historians derived Buchanan's and MacMillan's name from the O'Cahans. In his book *The Macmillans and their Septs* it was claimed that the Macmillans were descended from another root that may have come from the Iona area from one of the Irish monasteries. The second possible connection has already been mentioned. Angus Oge MacDonnell of the Isles had married Angus, daughter of Cooey of Norman times. She was said to have received a dowry of seven score men out of every surname under the O'Cahans. It was also supposed to cover the Monros, whose name derived from the fact that they came uppermost from the Roe waters. Their names were formerly O'Millan, etc. This derivation of the name Monro is a doubtful one. At this time Norman power was expanding in the Roe Valley, and there may have been a migration from the O'Cahans' territory to Scotland.

The position of the MacMillans in North Antrim is quite complicated. Some of the Scots colonizers who came across the North Channel either at the time of the plantation of Ulster or before may have changed their names to MacMillan under influence from the neighbouring O'Mullans. However, the O'Mullans may have had their name changed to MacMillan under the Scots influence from North Antrim. The Irish forces that attacked the Roe early in 1642 are said to have included McMillans. Name changes in North Antrim are still taking place.

The Scots MacMillans had settled for a while at Lough Tay in Perthshire. Some later migrated to Knapdale on the Argyll coast. Others went to Galloway and farms were established. John Macmillan was the founder of the Reformed Presbyterian Church. Alexander Macmillan, who came from the Isle of Arran, founded the publishing house of Macmillan fame. Another prominent figure was the lawyer and judge, Hugh P. Macmillan, who was created Lord Macmillan.

The name MacMillan is renowned in the United States, and it was brought there by one of Commander Peary's company on the expedition to the North Pole. MacMillan had great praise for the expedition, showing much bravery in the face of danger, and he later became a well-known Antrim explorer. E. M. McMillan discovered the element neptunium.

# Chapter 13

## *More about the Clans*

Let us glance back at the three sons of Owen, and to the genealogical chart. The *Tripartite Life of Patrick* mentions many blessings, said to have been given to Murdock, Fergus and Ochy Binny, son of Owen and grandson of High King Niall of the Nine Hostages. The blessings promised kingship to the descendants of Murdock. Clan Binny carried out the first attack into County Tyrone, described in Dr O'Kelly's book *Gleanings from Ulster History*. In it the history of the O'Neills and the MacLoughlins (who exercised kingship from Aileach and Tullyhog) is intertwined with Irish national history. There is the Clan Connor that emerged after a spell of division in Ulster. The period is dominated by the descendants of Fergus, son of Owen.

First of all let us deal with Clan Fergus; but there is not a lot of information available. Secondly there had been a lot of confusion between the Clan Fergus O'Mullans and the Clan Connor O'Mullans. Thirdly, some of the lands of the Clan Fergus territory in County Londonderry demarcated the territory of the Owen clan, and also embraced the Sperrin Mountains. North of the Sperrins lay the territory of the O'Cahans, McCloskeys and O'Mullans, of Clan Connor. South of the Sperrins lay the main territory of the O'Mullans, O'Hagans and O'Quins of Clan Fergus. They held land at the centre of the Owen kingdom around Tullyhog, south of present-day Cookstown.

From the Clan Fergus a liberal attitude towards religion was promised. The Church of Ireland in which they were to serve was part of the wider Catholic Church, but it preserved low-Church status. It had its own date for celebrating Easter, and its own liturgical forms. The clergy, however, were not strictly celibate; the Church was also monastic in form. The bishops of this Church seem to have been subject to abbots, and bishops were sometimes found living together to the number of seven. Aengus recorded 141 places in Ireland that had or had had seven contemporary bishops in one place. Numerous bishops followed the New Testament example of the apostles at Ephesus and Phillipi. The clan spirit entered mainly into the appointment of bishops and abbots as well as other clergy. In *The Life and Death of Saint Malachy the Irishman*, Saint Bernard wrote that they were a proud people, but they would not allow a bishop amongst them except one of their own class. They held the see of Armagh for 200 years, claiming it as their birthright.

In the two centuries following the death of St Patrick, Clan Fergus provided most of the prominent clergy. The Annals of the Four Masters records that Fiachna, a son of Fergus, became a bishop. It is through another son of Fergus, called Hugh, that the blessing of St Patrick seems to have taken place. Many of Hugh's descendants, Breacan, Colma and Becan rose to be bishops. The peak of activity came when MacLaisre of this family became an abbot or Archbishop of Armagh. The hold of the Oriella clan on the archbishopric was broken, and a representative of Clan Fergus was appointed to the highest office in the Gaelic Church. MacLaisre's descendants are given as the son of Luighdeach, the son of Ronan, the son of Tuadain, the son of Hugh, and the son of Fergus. MacLaisre died on 12 September AD 622, and was succeeded by Tomene, son of the Ronan already mentioned in the same high office. He is mentioned by the Venerable Bede in replying to the Roman Church about an accusation that the Irish Church was entertaining the Pelagian heresy. In later years the O'Mellans became prominent in ecclesiastical affairs.

Clan Fergus is not only famous for the two clergymen it produced, but also for its warriors. O'Dugan wrote a typographical poem about the various clans of Ireland, giving a large place to the race of Owen, of valiant arms, who had obtained the position of their greatness without fraud. O'Dugan wrote about the Clan Fergus, who were victorious over foes on all occasions. He praises the Siol Aedha or Children of Hugh, who were the descendants of Hugh, son of Fergus, with whom he had been dealing. Eanach is most likely the Enagh near Londonderry, which later became an O'Cahan stronghold, complete with castle on the island in Enagh Lough.

Clan Fergus probed south in the wake of Clan Binny into the heartland of Tyrone. Clan Binny has been described as the vanguard of the O'Neills and MacLoughlins as they fought their way towards Tullyhog and Armagh. When the Owen clan settled in Tyrone or Tir-Owen, the Land of Owen, the septs of the Clan Fergus obtained lands there. The lands of the O'Mellans (descendants of Hugh) were referred to as the Meallanaght, which included Slieve Gallion to the north of Cookstown. The O'Mullans' interest in Church affairs grew and they came into possession of a lot of Church lands. They were also the hereditary keepers of the Bell of St

Patrick, being the chief distinction of the O'Mullan clan. Another came into possession of the lands in the region of Donoughmore, north of Dungannon, where they were custodians of the Bell of Clogher. Another sept had moved nearer Armagh, where they ruled the territory of Lurga Ui Maellan.

There were two other clans descended from Coelbad, Hugh's brother: the O'Hagans and the O'Quins. The O'Hagans were the hereditary custodians of Tullyhog, the hill where the Kings of Ulster were inaugurated. O'Dugan wrote a poem which included a verse on the O'Hagans. Some of the O'Hagans were transported at a later date to lands lying north of the lands of the O'Mellans. The lands of the O'Quins and Clan Fergus appear to have been situated to the south-west of the O'Mellans in the vicinity of Lissan. There was another O'Quin in the area of Omagh, who should not be confused with the O'Quins of the Clan Fergus, since the Omagh O'Quins belonged to the Fir Magh Ithe.

The O'Hagans had an honoured position in the Clan Fergus. They played a leading role in the inauguration of the O'Neills described earlier. The position can be discerned from statements in the Annals. In 1081 the Annals of the Four Masters record that Magrath O'Hagan, Lord of Cinel Fergus, was killed. Under the date 1103 the Annals of Ulster record one Raghnall O'Hagan as 'the law giver of Tellach Og, who was slain by the men of Magh Ithe'. A further mention in the Annals of the Four Masters tells us that in 1122 an O'Hagan died. He was chief of Cinel Fergus and lawgiver of Tullyhog. The O'Hagan held the position of brehon or judge. The O'Hagan clan was the leading light in the Clan Fergus. As the Owen clan gradually expanded into the heartland of Ulster, Inishowen became more and more an outpost of the north. At length the political seat had changed from Aileach near Derry (Doire) to Tullyhog. Tullyhog was a place of importance from an early date. In AD 914, according to the Annals of Ulster, peace was declared at Tullyhog between the king of the province of Ulidia and the famous clan leader Owen, known as Niall Glundubh. At a later date Dungannon became the O'Neill headquarters, and their inauguration took place at that ancient seat of power, Tullyhog.

The O'Cahans were the custodians of the ancient Ulster site, and the O'Mullans were keepers of the venerable relic, the Bell of St Patrick, which may be as old as the fifth century AD. By far the greater number of books in the Gaelic or Celtic Church appear to have been portable, and to have been written by hand. These bells were cow and sheep bells, as used in present-day European countries. Ireland was perhaps the original land of these four-sided bells, and they have been found in many lands influenced by the early Irish Church, as far away as Brittany and Switzerland. A bell was a very important item presented to churchmen in the early Church in Erin, and these bells are often venerated and enshrined. They were rung down to modern times for the taking of oaths and for cursing. They were, however, not effective in drawing the Gaels to worship. The Bell of St Patrick, according to tradition, gave victory to its possessor over any enemy with whom he was engaged.

The Bell was held in great renown, and is illustrated by the following incident under the date 1044. The Annals of Ulster record that the son of the King of Aileach raided the Ui Meith and carried off 1,200 cows and a large number of prisoners in retaliation for the profonation of the Clocc-ind-Edecta (the Bell of the Testament). At length Tullyhog was desecrated, and this was followed by punishment. In this century there were considerable wars between the O'Neills and the McLoughlins to secure the Kingship of Ulster. In 1051 we discover that Ardgar McLoughlin, who was king, was expelled from the highship by Hugh O'Neill. However, Ardgar's son, Donnell, succeeded as King of Aileach in 1083, and he had held the kingship for eleven years. He later became High King of Ireland, a position which he held for twenty-seven years until his death at Derry in 1121. Donnell McCloughlin has been described as a most warlike man and the most capable ruler of his time. In the year 1111 a force was needed by the Ulidians to cut down many of its ancient trees. Neill McLoughlin disapproved and raided the Ulidians, carrying off 3,000 cows. Two years later Donnell McLoughlin at the head of a force deposed the King of Ulidia and retained a portion of its territory. He divided the remainder into two parts under petty chiefs. It was probably at this time that some of the O'Mellans came into possession of the lands of Kinel Awley, near present-day Banbridge.

Donnell McLoughlin caused a magnificent shrine to be made for the better keeping of the Bell of St Patrick. Donnell's name was inscribed on it and also the name of who was keeping the Bell at this time – one O'Mulholland. This name is also mentioned as keeper in 1365. But the Annals of 1356 record the death of Soloman O'Mellan, keeper of the Bell. In 1245 the keeper was an O'Mullan. The reason behind the two keepers is shrouded in mystery. Dr Kelly said that St Columba had discovered the Bell of the Testament in AD 552 in the saint's tomb according to the Annals of Ulster. The dual system of keepers may have been a compromise between the renown of St Patrick and the prestige of Columba. Another possibility is that the system of dual keepers may have been due to the struggles for power between the McLoughlins and the O'Neills and their supporters. Was the Bell entrusted to a keeper of one family, and then on the death of one of the keepers, did ownership fall to yet another keeper? Perhaps the Mulhollands and O'Mellans exercised a joint charge over the Bell, one keeping possession of it and the other entitled to use oaths.

The fight between McLoughlin and the O'Neills to gain possession of the title of the King of Ulster continued for some time. In 1167 it was recorded that the rivalry was settled temporarily by force from outside. The Annals of the Four Masters record that the men of Leinster and the Lords of Desmond and Thomond divided County Tyrone. The part with the mountain Slieve Gallon was given to Neill McLoughlin, while the southern half was given to Hugh O'Neill. The O'Neills eventually defeated the McLoughlins at the Battle of Caimeirge in 1241. Now the McLoughlins fall into obscurity and the O'Neills were to renew their importance until the plantation of Ulster. It is during this period of O'Neill ascendancy that the O'Mellans of Clan Fergus came into prominence. Their chiefs attained to positions of importance and great prestige in the kingdom. Other members followed the Church tradition. The O'Mellans were therefore frequently mentioned in the records of Church and state. Later we will reckon the role played by the O'Mellan.

The Annals of Lough Ce mention Bishop Thomas O'Mullan, who died in Rome in 1328. The Annals also, in 1336, mention the death of Soloman O'Mellan, keeper of the Bell of St Patrick. The event is also recorded in the Annals of the Four Masters. Soloman O'Mellan was acclaimed as a general patron of the clergy in Ireland. Another source mentions that he was the most illustrious of the clergy in Ireland. This emphasis upon O'Mullan as patron of the clergy in Ireland is not without significance. At this time the English churches of the Pale were putting forward their claims to support the status quo, a claim that had been given to them by the Pope. The church worked together with the civil authorities to promote English power and to destroy the power of the Gaelic chiefs. This encroachment as the order of things met with a lot of opposition from the chiefs and from the Irish clergy. The O'Mellans were prominent members of ecclesiastical resistance. Soloman O'Mellan earned the description of general patron of the clergy in Ireland.

The O'Mullans were also important in secular matters. The Annals of Ulster mentions them. The Ulster magnates went to meet the Earl of March at this time. The names mentioned are the O'Neills, Owen Roe O'Neill and O'Mullan, keeper of the Bell of St Patrick. O'Mullan now shared power with the high-ruling magnates.

During Donnell Owen's kingship, the O'Mellans were involved on his side in a disastrous battle in 1444. Owen O'Neill led a force of Ulster chiefs against the clan of Hugh Boy O'Neill. They had obtained independence in the area which was to become known as Clanaboy (Clan Aodh Boy). Their forces were beaten by the Clanaboy O'Neills and McQuillans, who wanted a large number of hostages. Including in the hostages was the son of the O'Mullans, which showed the continued importance of this clan. In 1455 Henry O'Neill took his father's place, and was declared king by O'Cahan, Mac Uidhir, Mac Mathgamna, and all the O'Neill clans and the successors of St Patrick. The reference made to 'the successors of St Patrick' shows the triumph of the English Church party. John Mey, the successor referred to, was the Archbishop of Armagh. Archbishop Mey arranged the traditional inauguration at Tullyhog, to be followed by a service at the Archbishop's residence at Armagh. The confirmation took place the following month and consisted of the imposition of hands by the Archbishop. These policies were declared necessary to bring the O'Neills within the compass of Church authority.

The O'Mellans played a leading role in the struggle between the Irish clergy and the poor English clergy. The Irish clergy are referred to as 'Inter Anglolicos'. The O'Mullans of the period were known as 'the turbulent O'Mullan'.

The O'Mullans had extensive lands in Central Ulster, including some Church and clan lands. They had also an important position and office among the Owen clan. In this way they were able to resist the English clerical encroachment in their area. Resistance gathered around Dean Charles O'Mullan. He was Dean of Armagh in 1430, and opposed attempts to further the aim of the pro-English ascendancy. However, he was removed from office and Dionysius O'Cullen of the Oriella clan ruled in his place. In 1441 the registrar of Archbishop Prene pronounced Dionysius Dean of Armagh and condemned Charles O'Mullan as the usurping body. The extent of Dean O'Mullan's support can be gauged by the sentences passed at the time upon John Connolly, Abbot of St Peter and Paul upon the Chancellor of the Prior of the Culdees in the rectories of Clonkarney and Clonfeale and on the vicars of Donoghmore, Termon, Argillkieran and Clonfeade. They were said to have aided and abetted the usurper O'Mullan. This gives us some idea of the powerful position in which Dean Charles found himself. In the same year, 1441, the Primate removed the keeping of the Bell of Saint Patrick from John O'Mullan, and conferred the charge upon the other keeper, Patrick Mulholland. The O'Mellans were therefore deprived of intruding into Church lands, and for failing to account for the revenue received from the Bell for the years 1417–41. In the following year Nachtan O'Donnell, chief of Donegal, with the Dean and Chapter of Raphoe, was excommunicated by the Primate because he had usurped, seized and detained the profits of the Bishopric of Raphoe. In both cases revenues raised locally were claimed by the central ecclesiastical authority.

The struggle was intense. Dean Charles O'Mullan played a leading part in the dispute. Owen O'Neill had also been involved, and in 1440 it was recorded that the Primate wrote to Owen, father of Henry O'Neill, Captain of the North, saying that Owen had sworn on the Baculum Jesus, in the Church of the Holy Trinity in Dublin, not to interfere with the Church's possessions. The Primate sent Phillip MacKewyn to him and O'Neill swore to make Charles O'Mullan dean. Culean was recognized the true and rightful dean. If not he was threatened with the secular authorities. The strongest arms in Ulster were the O'Neills.

In spite of the efforts to remove Charles O'Mullan, the clan seems to have won the battle. In 1446 Primate Boyle addressed Charles O'Mullan, Dean of Armagh, and the rest of the Armagh clergy, sending warrants against two of the O'Mullans. A quarter-century after the initial troubles and attempts to oust him, Charles O'Mullan rested secure in the deanery.

Toal and John O'Mellan were now in trouble. In 1446 Primate John Bole paid a visit to Armagh, the first visit paid by a Primate for nearly 200 years. This was like waving a red flag at a bull as far as the O'Mullans were concerned, for they did not forget that Archbishop Prens had deprived the O'Mullans of the custody of the Bell of St Patrick. Toal and John O'Mullan voiced their opposition to the visit of the Primate. In spite of their claim for clemency, as members of the ecclesiastical elect, he was publicly sentenced and the Deanery of Airhir placed under an interdict. From the time of Toal and John the history of the bell is obscure for many centuries.

Efforts to contain the O'Mullans were to no avail, and they continued to fill important places for the Clan Owen in the inauguration ceremony. In 1493 their importance came to the surface. There was a dispute over the succession of the O'Neill between Donnell and Henry, two brothers. Donnell was the eldest and was supported by the O'Donnells of Donegal. Now Henry the younger was inaugurated chief by O'Mellan and Sean O'Cahan, the fierce O'Cahan chief. According to the Annals the act was unlawful. The power of O'Cahan and O'Mellan was at its height.

At the end of the fifteenth century, and during the sixteenth century, there appears to have been a degree of development in that section of the O'Mullan sept based in County Armagh. The chiefs seem to have been differentiated from the O'Mullan himself by the addition of Oge in the name. In 1514 Felim Oge O'Mellan is mentioned, and also in 1600 when Owen Oge O'Mullan is recorded as chief of the sept. The Annals of the Four Masters in 1514 said that there was much fighting between the clans. They buried their dead. This was carried out by Hugh, son of Donnell O'Neill, and Con, the son of Niall. O'Neill and his friend MacDonnell had a strong body of troop. They routed the enemy and a descendant of Art O'Neill was amongst the slain. Hugh had lost two sons; the two slain were Felim Oge O'Mullan and Con O'Connor.

The O'Mellans of County Armagh had also been forced into the fight. They had extensive possessions in County Armagh, mainly Church lands. The name of O'Mellan at this time was changing, particularly in Armagh. The O had been dropped to a large extent and it had become Mellan. There were also changes in County Down and Tyrone. In County Down the name was sometimes spelt MacMullan, and even MacMillan. A number of the priesthood in County Down bore the name MacMullan and MacMillan. The O'Mellans are pointed to in some English records as O'Mullans. Queen Elizabeth said that the O'Mullans were those who followed the rebel Shane O'Neill in North Clanaboy, probably on his expedition against the MacDonnells.

The O'Mullans remained allied with the O'Neills in spite of developments, and the O'Neills had great faith in them. The Calendar of Documents relating to Ireland records in 1594 that an expedition on behalf of the Earl of Tyrone (O'Neill) was acting for the government against Connor Roe Maguire. The chief men involved in the expedition are recorded as O'Hagans, O'Quins and Patrick O'Mullan. These names were the chief septs of the Clan Fergus. From the same source it is learned that the Earl of Tyrone gave a pledge to the English. In 1600 it was also recorded that a spy reported to the English that Tyrone's daughter and O'Mullan's wife, were in Tyrone's camp. The camp was in the region of Muskerry, where O'Neill was fighting. There was a close relationship between the O'Mullan sept and the O'Neills, who were now Earls of Tyrone.

# Chapter 14

## *A Last Look at the Clans*

The story of the Ulster plantation throws a lot of light on the position and relations of the clans. Sir Arthur Chichester made some interesting statements and there were also statements by John Leigh, who was Sheriff of Tyrone in 1608. In the September of the same year, the state papers include Chichester's remarks on the position in Tyrone and Armagh. He said of Tyrone that he was a real menace, and goes on to say that the chief septs of the county are the O'Neills and under them the O'Donnells, the Mellans and other septs or tribes. These were warlike people and many of their number had to be provided for, so that they could rule their lands. Chichester went on to say that the state in Armagh was similar to County Tyrone, and possessed by the same tribes, notably that larger portion of the county ruled over the the Earl of Tyrone.

Leigh had given an interesting account of Tyrone. In it it recorded the division of the territory over which the O'Neill ruled. It showed that Hugh O'Neill, Earl of Tyrone, derived his support from Clan Fergus. Leigh had said that there had been certain kindreds of tribes of O'Neill in many parts of Tyrone who opposed Hugh O'Neill. All three of his septs and party, namely in the Barony of Strabane, had mixed feelings about English rule. In the Barony of Strabane, Oge O'Neill, son of Sir Arthur O'Neill, and his followers and dependants, along with the O'Neills and the O'Quins, hated Tyrone's sept and likewise in Clogher where there were two district septs of the O'Neills. They hated Tyrone and his tribes, one of whose septs was the son of Shane and his men. In the Barony of the Glynns the people consisted chiefly of the O'Neills, the O'Haggan, the Mulhollands with the McCahirs, and the Quins. They were totally dependent on the Earl of Tyrone and his septs, especially about that part of the barony called Killytragh, which was a fort. They inhabited the chief lands, and on lesser occasions they were the first to pull themselves in action for Tyrone's party. They were able out of their quarter to bring together at least 200 men, able and well armed within twenty-four-hours' warning. There was also the matter of the permitting of the natives, the Gaels, in every quarter of that county to boast the title of official for the bishop. This was a blow to the establishment of English laws amongst those barbarous people. This kind came under their local bishop and had taken up a position whereby all the quarrels and wrongs committed between the parties, in the name of the brehons or judges were examined. They, however, collected from the people at least three or four shillings in the pound as settlement.

Two septs of the O'Quins are cited. The Barony of Strabane was of different origins from the O'Quin of Clan Fergus, who held lands in the vicinity of Cookstown. The O'Mellans are sited by Leigh under the name of McCahirs. Cahir was a renowned name of the tribe O'Mellan around this period. His son, Fordorough McCahir, was pardoned for offences under the date 15 February 1607. Following Irish tradition, Leigh gave the sept the name O'Cahirs. From Leigh's report the O'Mellans, O'Hagans and others continued their life as brehons and judges, and administrators of oaths. They took advantage of the Protestant Church, which was in a state of unruly rebellion embracing all the Church lands. The Mulhollands also remain in sight and they must have secretly retained the Bell of St Patrick.

In the first part of the nineteenth century the Bell reappeared, after having been lost sight of for generations. At this time there died a schoolmaster called Henry Mulholland. One of his students had been Adam MacClean, who went into business at Belfast. As he was dying Henry sent for MacClean and gave him a box buried in the garden. When it was discovered it contained a woven copy of Bishop Bedell's Irish Bible, with the names of some of Henry's ancestors. It also contained that lost treasure, the Bell of St Patrick. Adam MacClean looked after the Bell during his lifetime. After his death his son sold it to Dr Todd of Trinity College Dublin. Upon Dr Todd's death, it was bought by the Royal Irish Academy for £500. It is displayed in the National Museum, Dublin.

The plantation or colonization would soon go on its own way. Leigh's account shows the enemy whom Hugh O'Neill had to confront on his own lands. In his book *Elizabethan Ulster*, Lord Ernest Hamilton said that the septs of the Clan Fergus, and particularly the O'Hagans, were the only ones that O'Neill had confidence in. The O'Hagans were O'Neill's foster brothers, who claimed royal descent as old as the O'Neills. The O'Donnellys had been a tribal sept of Shane O'Neill's. He supported Shane's son, who had opposed the Earl of Tyrone. The Flight of the Earls from Lough Swilly in 1607 removed O'Neill from Ulster.

Some of the Clan Fergus, loyal and trusted, went with the overthrown earl – among them were Shane O'Hagan and Murtagh O'Quin. Some numbers of Clan Fergus received lands, one being Cahir O'Mellan, who received a grant of one hundred acres in County Armagh. At Armagh the O'Hagans and two McQuins were granted small lots. In Tyrone, the Owen O'Hagan chief also received grants of land. Ferdoragh McCahir O'Mullen, chief of the O'Mellans, received sixty acres together with Phelemy MacMullan. His sons, Toal and Ferdoragh, received forty acres between them. A small number of the O'Quins and some others of the O'Hagans also received small grants of land. As has been pointed out they underestimated the lands actually received.

The state papers in 1611 gave a list of names, amongst whom was the Bargesses of Mountjoy, County Tyrone. One of the O'Mellans is included. He is named as John Mullane. The precinct of Mountjoy can also be mentioned. It was so called from the fort built in the territory. The change which was in progress in the name O'Mullan in Counties Armagh and Down has already been mentioned. In County Tyrone the name had already been changed from O'Mellan to O'Mullan, but more frequently to Mullan without the O. The English habit was to add an 'e' to the end of the name as seen in the above instance.

One of the saddest episodes of Irish history is the 1641 Rebellion. The O'Mellans have provided a connected narrative covering a number of years with Gaelic forces. The narrative was written by Friar Turlough O'Mellan of Nantry Friary,County Tyrone. He had been chaplain to Sir Phelim O'Neill, the Irish commander in the early years of the rebellion. The work has been widely acclaimed, and has been published in Irish in *Analecta Hibernica,* and read by Dr O'Donovan and others. An English translation from the Latin is available in *Historical Notices of Old Belfast*, edited by R. M. Young. O'Mullan in his work does not spare his own side. He is perhaps unkind in his condemnation of some of the clan names.

According to other contemporary writers, the O'Mellan's, O'Hagans, O'Quins and O'Mellans of Clan Fergus were very active in warfare. A writer on the period places them next to the O'Neills, amongst the leading clans engaged in the conflict, with an impressive list of names. The leading man of Clan Fergus in the 1641 Rebellion was Cormac O'Hagan, who was a competent commander. In his book on the Irish Rebellion, Lord Ernest Hamilton said that Cormac O'Hagan, while the most successful of Sir Phelim O'Neill's command in the north, was a humane man who would not be party to a massacre, especially of young children. He refers to Daniel O'Hagan in the same vein. Another O'Hagan commander, Shane, was captain of the fort at Toome. After more days of siege he was allowed to march out with all his men. But he was later captain at a battle near Letterkenny and was executed on the battlefield along with other persons of note. Hamilton comments favourably on the O'Hagan leaders. He goes on to say that the same humane treatment of women and children could not be attributed to the O'Quins and the MacVeighs. It mentions the name of the O'Quin commanders in connection with the massacre. In regard to the O'Mellans, Lord Hamilton records the adventures of Elsie Craig. She had been befriended and saved from the rebels by some of the clans.

As to the fighting, the armies of Cormac O'Hagan, comprising the O'Hagans, O'Mullans and O'Quins of Clan Fergus, along with the O'Cahans and O'Mullans of Clan Connor Magh Ithe, fought valiantly and won a number of battles. Rowley was defeated and his townlands taken over. A condition of the surrender was that one Conway was allowed to escape from the town along with its valuables, unimpeded by his own people. O'Mellan records that in 1643 Rory O'Hagan, the planter, assisted by the forces of Phillips of Limavady, proceeded to battle and was attacked by the O'Quins. Shane O'Hagan and his people were also attacked. Rory O'Mellan Ballagh was taken prisoner and Corr Criocach (Cookstown) was set ablaze. Cookstown, as he has been pointed out, was in O'Mullan territory, while O'Quin's territory was in the Lissan neighbourhood. Rory O'Mellan was coerced by the raiding forces. He was to act as an intermediary when demands were made of the Irish forces. These demands were refused. Patrick O'Mellan, son of Rory, has also been mentioned as a captain of the Gaelic forces.

In County Armagh, a number of the O'Mellans were captains in the armies of Sir Phelim O'Neill. Special mention is made of Captain Patrick O'Mellan, described as a gentleman in the depositions later taken in relation to the 1641 Rebellion. English writers have made much of the victory by Clothworthy over the O'Hagans, O'Quins and O'Mellans, with their allies. But there is another side to the story as pointed out by J. J. Marshall in his history of Mountjoy fort. Clothworthy marched out to attack the Irish forces, who refused to engage him in battle. He marched side by side at a safe distance. This astonished Clothworthy as recorded in O'Mellan's journal. The Irish had run out of ammunition and had sent a messenger to Galway with money to purchase more arms. The Irish now only made a pretence at resistance. Clothworthy learned these facts from a spy and now made an important ruse. To get close to the Irish, he ordered his men to remove their shirts to appear dressed as Irishmen in battledress. Clothworthy said that the Irish consisted of the O'Hagans, the Quins, the Mellans, the Neills of Killetra and the MacDonnells of the Earl of Antrim's country. They permitted Clothworthy's forces to infiltrate them. However, the Irish found out the strategy too late to avoid disastrous consequences. The 1641 Rebellion was drawn out. The hope of the Irish was that their commander, Owen Roe O'Neill, was an experienced commander. He died in 1649, so the Irish hopes faded away. A lament for him was written by the bards of Gall and Gael, who talked about doom and ruin — 'O great lost heir of the house of Niall'. This piece also applied to the cause of Owen Roe. After the fighting, the Civil Survey recorded that a number of those who had received lands at the plantation had been deprived of their part in the rebellion so that Hugh O'Hagan's sixty acres were declared forfeit, as were the forty acres of Towell McPhelemy McMellan and Ferdoragh McPhelemy McMellan.

What influence had these events upon the 1641 Rebellion? Hill gives an account of conditions of the clansmen in his *Plantation of Ulster*. He writes that the fate of such native gentry as were serviceable in numerous ways to the government were afterwards rewarded by small lots of barren soil, a long way from their houses. The plight was pitiable indeed. For them, and for those who had been cut out, the British settlers generally do not seem to have offered any sympathy. The winter of 1611 had set in, and few had their first crops saved. The Irish were in a demoralized state. The English settlers did not want a confrontation with the Gaelic churls. After November 1611, the Irish were doomed to transplant themselves. The supplanters were bound to have in readiness ample arms and ammunition — something that the Gaels were fully aware of. The Gaels had no reason to complain. Should anything untoward happen to them they persevered in wanting to hold on to their horses and lands. Any natives found lingering around premises that they owned could not expect a welcome. There were new bawns or castles. Not until the fateful winter of 1611 did the Irish appear to recognize the terrible horrors of their position: the full extent of their slavery and desolation.

The people that ruled Ulster now found themselves in a position of comfort and respect throughout the nine counties of the province. They were destined to become outcasts on their own soil, and their families were now likely to be lost. Their daughters, set to one side, were forced to marry beneath their rank. Some submitted peacefully to their destiny; others who held land were also constrained to live amongst the noblest of those who had been their fathers' tenants and servants. It had occurred to those involved that many of the gentry class, who were children in 1611, were in 1670 old men wearing frieze coats and favouring the land that had been granted to them in 1670.

However, not all the captured Gaels wanted to stay. When the conquest of Ulster was planned at the beginning of the seventeenth century Docwra learned at Londonderry the strange never-to-be-forgotten honking of the wild geese as they flew across the sky to unknown destinations. Darkness now fell over the Gaelic order. Numbers of young men of the Gaelic gentry class drifted to Europe in what became known as the 'flight of the wild geese'. In later years the younger sons of the Protestant ascendancy were also to come across the sea. Little tablets in chapels preserved the names of many who had died in distant lands or died on far-flung battlefields. But the wild geese were remembered because of their flight and were not usually remembered at home. There were other wild geese at work concerning the Wadding Papers of 1613–38. To the exiles Ireland was still home and they still took an interest in Church affairs from their places of exile. Some of them wrote that none but an Ulsterman should be appointed to the priory of Armagh. The Reverend Henry O'Mellan, along with others, was mentioned in regard to the priory.

Due to the troubled times records have been lost or destroyed. The struggle to survive was always to the fore, and this consumed so much energy that there was little left to preserve the past. Sometimes we have only traditions to rely upon, but this meant that events had been hazy as well as the coloured recollections of incidents long ago. Dr O'Donovan, according to one tradition, collected in South Derry deeds of O'Haran the plunderer. He had been appointed as a magistrate perhaps as a reward for his activities. O'Donovan tells of events and said that Francis Brollaghan told the story about Strad. Rory More O'Haran was to be the last of the Roman Catholic judges or JPs, who sat at Desertmartin. He ruled over territory of considerable extent and had his headquarters at Strad-Bally-Aran. Rory More O'Haran met his death riding through his lands, not many miles from his home. O'Mullan, who was in sight of him, came to his assistance at once and raised the horse out of the bog. Rory More thanked him and asked his name. The younger answered that it was no trouble. The grey-haired tyrant boasted that he had hung sixteen of the tribe. The youth was energetic and he was filled with indignation at the ingratitude of the wretches. He was seized head foremost into the slough out of which his horse had been saved. He said that he would never hang another of my name. O'Donovan recorded that the name as he found it used could equally be O'Mellan, for the name had been changed even earlier from the O'Mellan journal.

In the following year some of the Clan Fergus rose to fame. Of the O'Mullan sept Allen Mullan was born at Cookstown, graduated BA and MD at Trinity College, Dublin. The chief reason for his rise to fame was from *An Anatomical Account of Elephants*, written in the year 1681. He had sent letter to Sir William Petty, with the possibility of new astronomical equipment. He was elected fellow of the College of Physicians in Ireland, and was also a member of the Dublin Philosophical Society. He looked at the animals' ears and he was assisted in his efforts to research anatomy. He wrote interesting papers upon the subject with particular reference to the lens in his own eye. The life and work of Dr James Mullin, born in Cookstown in 1846, has already been mentioned. One Thomas Mathews wrote a book, *The O'Neills of Ulster*, in which it was claimed that the O'Mullans and the O'Quins were hereditary doctors in the Clan Owen.

The O'Hagans were hereditary lawgivers at Tullyhog during the Middle Ages. They had preserved something of their ancient traditions. Sir Thomas O'Hagan was a lawgiver in the family and was twice Lord Chancellor of Ireland. He was elected to the peerage in 1870, and took the title of Baron O'Hagan.

Some emigrants rose to fame in the United States as witness the financial wizard Andrew W. Mellan, who became Secretary to the Treasury in *"T. Mellan and His Times"*. He traced his family history back to Archibald Mellen, who settled on a farm near Newtownstewart, County Tyrone, about 1660. A judge claimed that an ancestor of Archibald's may have been an emigrant from Ulster, originating in Scotland.

Clan Connor Magh Ithe was also a noted name. The McCloskey family gave the United States an important politician. The O'Cahans or O'Kanes had filled places in the army and in the professions. Sport was the first love of these clansmen and it is worth stating that Barney Mullan, who played rugby for Ireland, had his origins in the clan homeland in County Londonderry.

We have witnessed the clan septs with their deep roots in Ulster's soil and past. We have observed their weakness, but also to pursue a fixed purpose. The clan system declined in the face of nationhood. The clan conflicts of the sons of Owen belong to another age. Their failures had not been in vain, and today they can be held in great veneration.

The turbulent past perhaps in the end has enriched our lives, as we have discovered the future of Ulster in her past and present.

# Select Bibliography

A. J. Hughes and R. J. Hannan, *Place-Names of Northern Ireland* (Institute of Irish Studies, 1992)

A. T. Q. Stewart, *The Shape of Irish History* (Blackstaff, 2001)

Colm Lennon, *Sixteenth-Century Ireland* (Gill & Macmillan, 1994)

S. J. Connolly (Editor), *The Oxford Companion to Irish History* (Oxford University Press, 1998)

David Ross, *Ireland: History of a Nation* (Geddes & Grosset, 2002)

G. A. Hayes-McCoy, *Irish Battles* (Appletree, 1989)

Ian Adamson, *The Ulster People* (Pretani Press, 1991)

Ian Adamson, *The Cruthin* (Pretani Press, 1974)

J. D. C. Marshall, *Dalriada* (Glenariff Development Group, 1998)

Liam de Paor (Editor), *Milestones in Irish History* (Mercier Press, 1986)

Michael Dolley, *Anglo-Norman Ireland* (Gill & Macmillan, 1972)

Maureen Donnelly, *The Nine Glens* (Donnelly, 2000)

Michael Richter, *Medieval Ireland* (Gill and Macmillan, 1988)

Michael Sheane, *Ulster and the Lords of the North* (Highfield Press, 1981)

Michael Sheane, *Ulster and the Middle Ages* (Highfield Press, 1982)

Michael Sheane, *Enemy of England* (Highfield Press, 1991)

Nick Constable, *Ancient Ireland* (Promotional Reprint Company, 1996)

R. F. Foster (Editor), *The Oxford History of Ireland* (Oxford University Press, 1989)

Rosemary Evans, *The Visitor's Guide to Northern Ireland* (Blackstaff, 1998)

Sean McMahon, *A Short History of Ulster* (Mercier Press, 2000)

T. H. Mullin and J. E. Mullan, *The Ulster Clans* (North-West Book, 1966)